DATE DUE			
JUL 7 '88			
3 03 1988			
MAY 2 8 1989			
AUG 1 6 1989			
NOV 0 4 1993			
DEC 1 6 1997			

FRANCE REVIEWS ITS
REVOLUTIONARY
ORIGINS

FRANCE REVIEWS ITS REVOLUTIONARY ORIGINS

SOCIAL POLITICS AND HISTORICAL OPINION IN THE THIRD REPUBLIC

By PAUL FARMER

OCTAGON BOOKS

A DIVISION OF FARRAR, STRAUS AND GIROUX

New York   1973

Reprinted 1963
by special arrangement with Columbia University Press

Second Octagon printing 1973

OCTAGON BOOKS
A DIVISION OF FARRAR, STRAUS & GIROUX, INC.
19 Union Square West
New York, N. Y. 10003

LIBRARY OF CONGRESS CATALOG CARD NUMBER: 63-20890
ISBN 0-374-92698-0

Printed in U.S.A. by
NOBLE OFFSET PRINTERS, INC.
New York, N.Y. 10003

PREFACE

No HISTORICAL PROBLEM has more meaning for our own times than that raised by the great French Revolution. The crisis that marks French politics in this generation is fundamentally the continuation of a struggle begun in the last decade of the eighteenth century; it was then that its elements first appeared and that their relationships were first indicated. And the forces revealed in this process are common to the experience of all the European nations.

Probably no treatment of that subject can fully measure up to its potentialities. Certainly the brief analysis presented here falls far short of doing justice to its material.

This study attempts to account for the persistence among historians of an irreconcilable conflict over the significance of the French Revolution, in spite of an increasing factual knowledge of the event. The more this paradoxical situation is considered, the more its importance is appreciated. It becomes clear that an answer to why men disagree over the meaning of the Revolution goes far to identify the moving forces in French and European history since then. It likewise appears that the same answer implies much concerning the nature of historical study.

To the degree that the present work reveals the importance of its problem, its own shortcomings are exposed. But it is offered in the hope that it will suggest much of what it omits and that it will forward an understanding of why men still are divided over the issues of the Revolution.

A study such as this, dealing with the manner in which historical judgments are formed, can not but make the author acutely aware of the extent of his own indebtedness. A wide range of people bear responsibility, for better or worse, in the present work; their number includes many far removed from any direct contact with it.

Acknowledgement is gladly made of the guidance given by Professor Carlton J. H. Hayes of Columbia University, under whose direction this study was begun, and of the invaluable help given by Professor Shepard B. Clough of Columbia University in overcoming difficulties that arose in carrying it to completion. For the assistance and encouragement given me by Professor Charles W. Cole, both at Amherst College and at Columbia University, there can be no adequate expression of my appreciation.

The period of study of which this small volume is a first product would have been impossible without the generous grants of scholarships and fellowships by Amherst College and Columbia University.

PAUL FARMER

Hamilton, New York
September, 1943

CONTENTS

CHAPTER ONE

HISTORY *AS* PRESENT
POLITICS

THE HISTORIOGRAPHY of the French Revolution occupies a position in the field of historical writing quite as remarkable as the place which the events of the Revolutionary era hold in the development of the modern European world.

Because the Revolution so markedly influenced the shape of things to come and because the issues it embodied remain of such vital importance, it has been studied with an intensity seldom equaled. Even while the Revolution was still in mid-course, it gave rise to a flood of historical writing which continues unabated to the present day.

The historical study of the Revolution has developed in France into a large-scale industry, supplying an important public need. Every remaining evidence of the Revolution has been preserved and made available to research. Learned journals and societies—provincial, national, and international—are dedicated solely to the study of the Revolution. The great expenditure of private and public resources on this work has been matched in human terms by the many scholars who have spent their whole lives in the investigation of this one field.

Despite the great effort which has been devoted to the study of the Revolution during the past one hundred and fifty years, historians have not come to agreement in their findings. The Great Revolution cut a sharp line through French society. Before the Revolution had even reached its peak, the nation was clearly divided into those who supported and those who opposed it. That line has never been effaced, nor has it been obscured by the lesser disagreements on either side of the major division. Since the beginning of the nineteenth century, there has been not one France, but two, and the beginning of a third. Revolutionary historiography began as a continuation of the conflicts which had been expressed in the Revolution itself, and these contradictions have remained an integral part of historical writing on the Revolution ever since.

The controversy over the history of the Revolution is distinguished from other unsettled historical problems in that judgments on the Revolution serve as the locus of almost all the divisions of opinion in France on the problems of modern life. Historical interpretations are inseparably joined to alignments on contemporary politics, to corresponding opinions on such questions as the interrelationships of the state, the individual, religion, society, and classes, and to corresponding evaluations of nationalism, tradition, and the Church. A particular position on the history of the Revolution implies a particular attitude on most other public questions, and these, in turn, are customarily referred to the Revolution as a major premise. This practice has become so much a convention of French intellectual expression that historical judgments on the Revolution constitute a natural and proper subject even for debates in Parliament. The body of historical writing on the Revolution thus apparently presents the paradox of an exhaustive study of a large mass of material which, instead of producing an informed agreement on the subject under investigation, perpetuates the conflict in judgment on the Revolution and reflects the basic cleavages on contemporary public problems.

The historian who turns his attention to the development of France since the Revolution is forced in view of this situation to consider the historiography of the Revolution, quite apart from any immediate interest in the events of the Revolutionary epoch itself, as a distinct and important part of post-Revolutionary French history. It is this role of historical judgment on the Revolution in the modern history of France which forms the subject of the present study.

Several possible approaches to the problem lie open to investigation. Revolutionary history presents, in the first instance, the occasion for historiographical criticism. The process by which historical knowledge of the Revolution has been accumulated and refined might well be reconstructed and examined. The task would entail a chronological study of writings on the Revolution in order to trace changes in historical opinion, shifts in emphasis, alterations in the purposes which historians set themselves, controversies among historians, the growth of the fund of factual knowledge, and the extent to which historians approached agreement in their interpretations. Such an inquiry would further be concerned with the development of technics of historical study, the utilization and control of sources, public and private projects for the study of the Revolution, and the establishment and careers of historical societies and journals.

Or a full-scale history of France might be oriented about the controversy over the history of the Revolution. The Revolution, as a body of doctrines, was subjected to continual criticism as its implications touched on every important aspect of public life. Attitudes towards the Revolution controlled a major part of the conflicts over constitutional law, religious policy, education, social philosophy and politics, diplomacy, and almost all questions of the day. These problems might well be considered from the Revolution as a point of reference. Such an analysis would trace within these diverse fields the continuing influence of the Revolutionary tradition, the interplay of the individualist, authoritarian, and egalitarian elements within it, the course of the opposition to the Revolutionary doctrines, and the development of these few forces which have neither a Revolutionary nor a counter-Revolutionary tradition. A study so organized would throw a revealing light on the recent history of France.

A third approach to the same body of material would center in the philosophy of history. The historiography of the Revolution presents in most striking fashion the basic questions of the nature of historical study. Historical writing on the Revolution has served as an innocent pastime, a form of artistic expression, an exhortation and a polemic, and an attempt to ascertain scientific truth. Which of these has truly been history, and what do these efforts show of the proper function of history? If the function of history is to discover objective truth, as it is commonly assumed to be, how can it be demonstrated that objective truth can be reached, since the tremendous labor spent on the study of the Revolution has not resulted in agreement on the most important problems involved? These questions, which stand out most clearly in the historiography of the French Revolution, underlie the whole discipline of historical research, and the nature of historical writing itself might well be illustrated in the case of the history of the Revolution.

The present study is not based on any of these approaches. But these alternative methods of utilizing the same material must be mentioned here, for they are necessarily suggested in the subsequent development of the present project.

The investigation which is here undertaken sets itself this task: to trace the course of historical judgment on the chief questions of interpretation in the historiography of the French Revolution; to illustrate the manner in which these interpretive judgments form part of particular systems of social politics; and to indicate that both the historical judgments and the ideologies of which they form a part are controlled by the social experience of the groups which support them and by the movement of social forces within the life of modern France.[1]

Because the quantity of historical writing on the French Revolution is far too great to be dealt with exhaustively, it is necessary to set somewhat arbitrary bounds to the material which is to be considered. This study is limited, first, to formal historical accounts of the Revolution, as distinguished from writings aimed at other purposes which refer to the Revolution only incidentally; and then, to those historical accounts which were written in France during the Third Republic.

Within this range, the approach to the problem leads to a further selection of the material to be examined in detail. The present study is concerned primarily with establishing the manner in which historical judgments on the Revolution were controlled by social forces active in the Third Republic; those historical works are most relevant, therefore, which were not confined to the scholarly world but which received widespread public attention and support. Monographs, learned journals, and scholarly polemics all left their marks on the development of historical thought. But these contributions of research ordinarily became public property and merged into the unending conflict over the Revolution which was being waged in public life, only as they were presented to the general public in full-dress histories of the

Revolution published by writers whose works were widely read. Chief attention will therefore be given to the general histories of the Revolution which first appeared during the Third Republic and which received widespread public acceptance.

The intellectual biographies of the historians themselves are of comparatively little importance for the purposes of this study. Correspondences appear between the interpretations presented in the widely read histories and the social experience of large sections of French society. Whether the historian was conscious of this relationship and intended that his work should lend support to one side or another in public controversy is of small significance. The public character of his work would not be governed by the historian's attitude towards it, for the thousands who read his work and either acclaimed it or denounced it would do so on the basis of the published text, not the author's private intentions.

Because this study is concerned primarily with the expression of social forces in the historical interpretation of the Revolution rather than the internal history of historical writing on the Revolution, the scheme by which it is organized depends on the development of French national life rather than on the course of Revolutionary historiography. The historical works to be considered are treated in four groups. The first, which includes the major works published before the Third Republic, serves to indicate the state of historical writing on the Revolution at the outset of the period under study. The three other divisions are marked out by stages in the development of the Third Republic.

The progress of historical judgment on the Revolution before 1871 serves, for the purpose of the present study, only as a background to the work of the Third Republic. The earlier historians therefore receive only a brief treatment. Although a general correspondence between the histories of the Revolution and contemporary political and social circumstances is immediately apparent, no attempt is made to examine in detail the relationship between the historians and their times. Only a broad outline is presented of the state of historical opinion on the Revolution at the point from which the historians in the Third Republic took their start.

The first two decades of the Third Republic derive a unity from the overshadowing struggle to establish the Republic or, conversely, to destroy it. The proclamation of the Republic may be an arbitrary beginning for this period, but it has a real termination in the decade of the 1890s. The publication of H. A. Taine's history of the Revolution was one of the first-rank events in the intellectual history of these times. His attack on the fundamentals of the Revolution set the Revolutionary historiography in the Third Republic apart from that preceding, shifted the alignment of forces in the controversy over its significance, and became the basis for a conservative school of thought which lasted throughout the Republic. Taine's attack was met by a republican defense of the Revolution. No single history of the Revolution was written during the early Republic in support of this tendency, but it was expressed in several series of historical studies which appeared in Gambetta's journal *La République française* and were later reprinted. The publication of Albert Sorel's work some years later, although it diverged in some respects from the republican historical conventions, further supported the position of the left. The conflicting interpretations of left and right which were thus expressed were intimately bound to the social and political philosophy of the groups interested either in furthering or in impeding the contemporary progress of republicanism, and both antagonisms arose from the same historical circumstances.

The two decades before the first World War constitute one of the most important periods of French life. A whole set of forces which had been developing since early in the nineteenth century emerged into the forefront of French history during the decade of the 1890s and fundamentally transformed the life of the French nation. Then, in 1914, French history was interrupted and merged into the history of the European world at war. Historical continuity was sustained in these pre-war years by the works of Alphonse Aulard and Louis Madelin, who reformulated the traditional interpretations of left and right. The changes characteristic of the times reveal their impact in the modifications of the left and the right produced in the socialist history of Jean Jaurès and in the incomplete work of Augustin Cochin.

The history of the Third Republic in its last twenty years was dominated by the continuing crisis which the first World War had precipitated and which centered in the fate of traditional republicanism, now
beset both by an antirepublican right and by a socialist left. This situation is paralleled in the centrist position of republican historiography
of the Revolution, flanked by a socialist interpretation which was supported by the work of Albert Mathiez, and by an antiparliamentary
conservative school of which Pierre Gaxotte was a spokesman.

CHAPTER TWO

BEFORE THE THIRD REPUBLIC

THE SEVENTY years of the Third French Republic mark off the period with which the present investigation is chiefly concerned. The Third Republic comprises a real unity, for the problems of French society during its lifetime were commonly expressed in issues which were drawn from the implications of republican government. But the political revolutions, including that of 1870–1871, which hold the foreground of nineteenth-century French history, obscure a continuity that is quite as important as the constitutional changes—the fundamental constancy of French social life during the greater part of the nineteenth century.[1]

An equilibrium was reached in France, perhaps as early as 1800 and surely by 1815, when the Revolution had reached its peak and then receded as far as it was destined to. The Revolutionary epoch had demonstrated that neither the old aristocracy nor the new bourgeoisie could govern by itself. The working partnership between the two groups which was established by the time of the Bourbon Restoration proved to be lasting. The terms and the respective influence of the partners were often subjected to dispute, and this contributed largely to the constitutional crises of 1830, 1848, 1850–1852 and later. But France was governed by this partnership down almost to the end of the century.

This element of stability rested on the comparatively slow but steady progress of the industrial revolution in nineteenth-century France. Technological advances were increasingly absorbed, to be sure, and they worked an alteration in the underlying character of the economy: industrial production was accelerated, the unification and expansion of the home market was further advanced, and population was slowly transferred from the countryside to the cities and towns. French economic life experienced increased changes, which developed at an irregular rate as they were affected by the fluctuations of the business cycle. But the transformation did not reach revolutionary proportions before the end of the century. France remained a rural and agricultural nation with an important but relatively small-scale industrial and commercial life.

The steady movement of French life was so greatly transformed during the 1890s that this decade marks a more important division in French history of the century than any of the political revolutions.[2] The change can not be sharply defined. It was not a matter of innovation: most of the elements had their origin early in the century. It was not closely associated with a date: some of the developments matured before 1890, some not until the new century. But within a relatively short interval, French industry began to expand at an unprecedented rate and assumed a more decisive importance than agriculture, a new imperialism took hold of France, nationalism was heightened and expressed in new forms, the socialist movement became strongly entrenched, the relations of Church and state were basically altered, and the pre-eminence of scientific methods was extended to new fields of thought. The first two decades or so of the Third Republic therefore reveal more in common with the preceding years of the nineteenth century than with the period which began in the 1890s.

The development of historical interpretation of the Revolution follows a similar pattern.

The Third Republic forms, in the main, a distinct and coherent period in Revolutionary historiography. In the early years of the Republic, the array of historical judgments underwent a considerable shift from positions developed in the preceding fifty years. Controversy over the interpretation of the Revolution proceeded thereafter from the new bases.

But there is also a continuity in historical writing on the Revolution which extends from the early years of the century down into the Third Republic and is then extinguished sometime about 1890. The Republic inherited much from the earlier period. Several of the histories written during the preceding half-century remained current during the 1870s and for some time afterwards. The historians of the time carried on the pioneer labors of their predecessors in studying the sources and were indebted to them for developing a number of points of interpretation. The tone of historical writing during the early years of the Republic is related, too, to that which went before. Historical writing from the Bourbon Restoration until well into the Third Republic was frankly presented as a mixture of literature and political argument. Although the fundamental importance of the documentary record was universally acknowledged, many historians troubled themselves little with its study. But this approach to history was vanquished near the turn of the century with the triumph of the movement to bring historical method into closer relation to that of natural science. The efforts of historians were turned chiefly to detailed study of the sources and to monographic controversy, and history became more of a profession and less of a political avocation. As a consequence, the historians during the early years of the Republic have more in common with those of the preceding fifty years than with the academic historians at the end of the century.

The outstanding works on the Revolution published during the earlier generations must therefore be reviewed briefly before attention is given to the developments which came during the Third Republic.[3]

The years immediately following the Revolution brought the publication of a quantity of memoirs and reflections on the Revolution written by men who had figured in it. Many of these early writings bear an historical character in so far as they are critical reviews of the Revolutionary period, but they either do not treat the Revolution as a whole or do not present a consecutive narrative. They serve chiefly as preparations for the full historical accounts which came later.

One of the most notable of these early treatments was written by Mme de Staël (1766–1817), the distinguished daughter of Necker. Mme de Staël's work, *Considérations sur la Révolution française,* was published in 1818, the year after her death.[4] The wide renown of the author, resting on her prominent position in French society and on her accomplishments as a writer, sufficed to gain a large audience for her work on the Revolution. But the attention which it received was due as well to the extent to which the volumes, published in the first flush of the Bourbon Restoration, defended the basic features of the Revolution.

The old monarchy had maintained its government without any sort of constitution, in Mme de Staël's view, and thereby denied the nation a fundamental right. The historical process by which the monarchy had become absolute, furthermore, had extinguished a real body of liberties which the nation had formerly enjoyed. The Revolution, which arose from these circumstances, was therefore a product of the history of the old monarchy itself and, in large measure, was justified by it. Such a work, appearing at a time when the Bourbons were endeavoring to efface the memory of the Revolution and setting itself against the defense of traditionalism then being established by Bonald, de Maistre, and Chateaubriand, was viewed as a bold defense of the Revolution and marked a recession of support from the Restoration.

The first two full-length histories of the Revolution appeared about five years after Mme de Staël's *Considérations* had stirred Restoration society. They passed well beyond her defense of the Revolution to strike a direct blow at the Bourbon monarchy. A liberal opposition was gaining ground, especially within sections of the middle class, which looked forward to strengthening the power of Parliament within the monarchy. The first formal histories of the Revolution were written with the clear purpose of utilizing the events of the Revolutionary era to discredit the Bourbons and justify the cause of constitutional monarchy.

The two young liberals who wrote these histories, F. A. Mignet (1796–1884) and Adolphe Thiers (1797–1877), were close friends. Mignet had come to Paris in 1821, after winning distinction for a study of the institutions of Saint Louis. Thiers made his entry into the political life of the capital in the same year. The two men became associated with the founding of the *National* as an opposition journal and, as editors, both took prominent parts in the resistance to the press laws that precipitated the Revolution of 1830. The friendship which

Thiers and Mignet formed in these years lasted throughout their careers, the one as a political leader under the Orleans monarchy and the Third Republic, the other as an historian.

Their two histories of the Revolution appeared about the same time. Thiers's work was published in ten volumes, between 1823 and 1827.[5] While this was being issued, Mignet published his much briefer account in 1824.[6] Both works found a ready market and sold widely. The popularity of Mignet's history proved more lasting, and it was reprinted at frequent intervals throughout the century and even as late as 1914.

The viewpoint expressed in the two works was much the same. The Revolution was presented as a movement arising out of the requirements of the times and proceeding with a force which overrode the powers of individual figures. Its development was unfortunately marred by violence and excess, but in its sum it brought much more benefit to France than evil. Both the benefits, which represent the core of the Revolution, and the evils to which it proved subject, demonstrate the necessity for a liberal monarchy which would establish government by representatives of the nation and, at the same time, exert a restraining authority.

The current state of historical interest was reflected in the next major work on the Revolution to appear, the forty-volume miscellany published by Buchez and Roux between 1834 and 1838.[7]

The early nineteenth century was notable for an especially large concern with historical writing. This was manifested in the readiness with which a wide public audience was secured for bulky historical works which ran into many volumes. It was marked, as well, by the effort expended in collecting source materials and preparing them for study. Among the enterprises of this sort undertaken at this time was the publication, in various series between 1822 and 1834, of all the laws and decrees in French history. Such projects received influential support when Guizot, himself an historian, took office under Louis Philippe. He was instrumental in starting the publication of the vast *Collection de documents inédits sur l'histoire de France,* which includes a series dealing with the Great Revolution. Guizot was largely responsible, too, for the revival of the *Académie des sciences morales et politiques* in 1833, which shortly thereafter began the publication of its *Bulletin* and its *Annuaire historique*. In 1833 the *Société de l'histoire de France* was also founded and its series of publications begun. The study of the Revolution received particular assistance ten years later from the reprinting of the *Moniteur,* for long the main source for the daily proceedings of the legislative bodies of the Revolutionary period. The *Histoire parlementaire* of Buchez and Roux was related to this trend, for it is as much a source collection as an interpretive treatment. It consists of a mass of speeches, budgets, proceedings of assemblies and clubs, reports of debates, and other documents, bound together by narrative passages which feature the distinctive social views of Buchez.

P. J. B. Buchez (1776–1860) had been a Carbonaro and then a follower of Saint-Simon before he worked out his own social philosophy. This was built on a conception of progress through a succession of historical stages and retained a similarity to the doctrines of Saint-Simon. But Buchez held firmly to Christianity and Catholicism, and in his presentation the last stage of progress was the Christian era. This epoch would be fulfilled when the principles of Christianity received complete expression in society. The ultimate social order would fuse democracy, Catholicism, and a kind of socialism.

The interpretation of the Revolution which Buchez rested on this Catholic social democracy strongly favored the cause of the revolutionaries. Although Buchez deplored the violence which frequently accompanied the crises of the Revolution, his support of it extends into the period of the Convention and the Terror. His treatment of Robespierre shows a real, if distant, respect for the man who led the Revolution at its most extreme phase, even though his policy is criticized from the standpoint of Buchez's own doctrines. But Buchez's social philosophy stood apart from the main currents of opinion of the time, and the position which his work secured was due more to the diligence with which it assembled an important body of information on the Revolution than to the interpretation it offered.

A justification of constitutional monarchy supported by the history of the Revolution appeared again, after Thiers and Mignet, in the work published by François Droz in 1839–1842, but Droz's account was much more carefully prepared than theirs had been.[8] Droz (1773–1850), a liberal who had secured some prominence as a writer on philosophy and political science, had been a witness of the development of the Revolution and then had spent more than thirty years in the study of its history, examining documents and interviewing survivors. He was primarily interested in establishing that the failure of Louis XVI and his ministers to concede the needful demands of the Revolution and then take over leadership of it resulted in the extension of the Revolution to the extreme and violent forms it eventually assumed. His three volumes are accordingly confined to the events of 1789 and the career of Mirabeau.

A new direction was given to the interpretation of the Revolution with the development of a considerable republican movement during the later years of the reign of Louis Philippe. The outstanding works so far published had been moderate defenses of the Revolution, in support of limited monarchy. Buchez was a republican, to be sure, but his distinctive social views were not widely shared. But three histories of the Revolution which gained wide acceptance and were to fulfill the same function for republicanism that those of Thiers and Mignet had performed for the Orleans monarchy began to appear in 1847. Two of them were written by men who were to play prominent parts in the Revolution of 1848—Lamartine and Louis Blanc; the third, that written by Michelet, won an overshadowing popular esteem which was to last throughout the century.

Lamartine's *Histoire des Girondins,* although it had only a relatively short life as an historical work, served well at the time of its publication as a political weapon directed against the Orleans monarchy and in support of republicanism.[9] Lamartine (1790–1869) came of a wealthy and noble royalist family. His reputation as a romantic poet he quickly won during the 1820s. He entered Parliament under the Orleans monarchy as a Legitimist. But with the passage of time his antagonism to the Orleanists led him to support the republican forces, and he gave expression to a kind of liberalism which advocated democracy, separation of Church and state, and social reform within the bounds of private property.

Lamartine's study is not limited by its title and actually covers, in its fashion, the course of the Revolution as far as the Thermidorean reaction. The Girondins stand out as proponents of that democratic and humanitarian liberalism which Lamartine considered to be the legacy of the Revolution and which formed part of the republicanism of 1848. Lamartine himself presented Robespierre in terms almost as favorable as those in which he eulogized the Girondins. But the noble character which he attributed to the Girondins was for long afterwards contrasted to that of the Montagnards to the discredit of the latter.

The republicanism of the first half of the nineteenth century was compounded of several loosely joined elements. The men of 1848 shared common aspirations for a peaceful state in which the people would rule themselves and all men would be joined together in works of humanitarian social reform, in recognition of the underlying brotherhood of man. One wing of the movement looked forward to a republic which would fulfill these purposes within the limits of middle-class liberalism. But the republicanism of 1848 embraced as well an element which required something other than liberalism to meet the demands of social fraternity. This group did not clearly define its program, but rejected competition as a basis of society and put its hopes in a co-operative society of producers.

While Lamartine was one of the prominent figures in liberal republicanism, Louis Blanc was the leader of the socialist group. A career as a journalist had brought Louis Blanc (1811–1892) to the position which he enjoyed in 1848 as spokesman for the extreme left. His reputation rested not only on his newspaper work but on a number of books which he had written in support of producers' co-operatives and social credit. It was in consideration of these views that he was made a member of the provisional government in 1848. But his project for national workshops gained only ineffective support and provoked a strong opposition, and they failed to accomplish the purposes he had set for them. When the political power of the working class was broken and the republican forces were purged of their left wing, he was arraigned for trial and forced to flee to England.

During his exile in England, Louis Blanc continued to work on the history of the Revolution which he had begun to publish in 1847. He brought the work to completion in 1862.[10] His interpretation of the Revolution reflects his position in the republican movement. As he viewed it, the long struggle against authority, of which the Revolution was the highest stage, manifests two divergent tendencies. One trend is towards individualism: this is a corruption of liberty. The other moves towards fraternity as its goal: this is the true culmination of liberty. While the middle class held control of the Revolution in its early phases, from the National Assembly through the period of the Gironde, the current was towards individualism. But when the Montagnards came to power as the champions of the people, the Revolution was transformed from a system for the protection of the bourgeoisie into a defense of the common people. The violence and severity of the Terror, which give it its name, were unfortunate, but they must be understood in relation to the dangers confronting the Revolution. Robespierre himself, who embodied the Revolution, was neither callous nor naturally tyrannical; he only yielded to the temptation to use bloody means for the achievement of a laudable purpose.

The third of the republican histories of the Revolution which began to appear in 1847 was written by a professional historian of the first rank.[11] Jules Michelet (1798–1874) devoted his career entirely to the teaching and writing of history. His work was distinguished by a highly colored and imaginative treatment of broad ranges of material, and he secured a wide popular audience. He had established his reputation by a summary of modern history in 1827 and an introduction to universal history in 1831. Michelet, whose antagonism to the government of Louis Philippe had already led him into several political sorties, set aside his other work in order to present a history of the Revolution which would reveal the virtues of republicanism and assist in replacing the Orleans monarchy. But the Republic had been reestablished and again overthrown before he finished his writing in 1853, and the last volume appeared after the author, in disfavor with the government of the Second Empire, had been constrained to retire to Nantes.

The history of the Revolution which Michelet offered quickly won a place in popular esteem which it has not yet entirely lost. It was still being reprinted in the early years of the twentieth century. Its position rests largely on the manner in which Michelet presented the people of France themselves as the protagonists of his account. The Revolution was not, for Michelet, so much an external sequence of events as an expression of the ideas of peace, justice, and fraternity which lie in the hearts of the people. The great days of the Revolution were the outward sign of the power and virtue of the French people. The massacres and the Terror, which hold so large a place in the events of the period, were not the work of the people, but of the individuals who for the moment had seized control of the movement; of those who bear responsibility for this perversion of the Revolution, Robespierre was chief. The ideas of the Revolution and the beneficent power of the people receive their natural expression in the republic. They imply, in addition, a contradiction to the power of the Church. Michelet's history thus summed up the features of anticlericalism and the democratic exaltation of the people which were to remain central elements in the republican interpretation of the Revolution.

During the Second Empire, the character of historical study of the Revolution underwent several modifications. Histories of the Revolution ceased to be so intimately bound to immediate political conflicts as they had been at first. The histories, from Mignet and Thiers to Michelet, which had secured widest audience and influence in the early years of the century, had been conceived and received as incidents in the current political struggles, and had exerted considerable influence in determining them. The histories which received comparable attention in later generations held just as real political implications, but they did not stand in quite so direct a relation to the issues of the day.

Research on the Revolution also put a new emphasis on the study of the contemporary sources. Intensive work of this sort, indeed, was really begun during this period. The earlier historians had had to rely largely on the memoirs which first became available as the survivors of the Revolution reached old age and as private papers and collections were made public. The task of examining the documents which dated from the Revolutionary epoch itself received increasing attention during the Second Empire as larger bodies of material were made available to study, and historians seriously began the almost endless work of exploring collections on the Revolution, especially those in provincial archives. This absorbed an increasing amount of effort until, by the middle of the Third Republic, it became the dominating historical occupation. Among the most notable of these works of archival research to appear during the Second Empire were the study of the Terror begun by Mortimer-Ternaux and carried on by Henri Wallon, the extended biographical defense of Robespierre written by Ernest Hamel, and Alexis de Tocqueville's analysis of the relationship between the old regime and the Revolutionary.

The new stage in Revolutionary historiography was further revealed with the publication of Tocqueville's study in 1855, for his analysis of the Revolution showed less sympathy for it than had any of the other accounts which attained foremost renown in the half-century before the Third Republic.[12] The success of Tocqueville's work may be attributed in large part to the disillusionment induced in some quarters by the events of 1848–1852. The historians who had been most heeded during the Orleans monarchy had presented republicanism as the true fulfillment of the Revolution and as the incarnation of justice and liberty. But when the Republic was established for a second time, its course ran parallel to that of the first by eventuating in what some groups considered to be disorder and dissolution of society, and it was replaced by a Bonapartist autocracy. An atmosphere was thus created which would give favor to a more severely critical examination of the Revolution.

Tocqueville, in particular, gained in public repute from this situation, for he had earlier expressed views on the nature of democratic government which seemed now to be confirmed. Tocqueville (1805–1859) had begun his public career as a royalist. He held office as a deputy under the Orleans monarchy and as Minister of Foreign Affairs in the Second Republic. But his name had been made by a study of American democracy which he had published in 1835–1840, on his return from a visit to the United States. He considered democracy to be a growing force, so strong that it could not be denied. Yet unchecked, it tended towards excessive authority and centralization. In order to preserve liberty, therefore, democracy must be restrained by the separation of powers. His position was thus not one of direct opposition to democracy, but of an eminently reserved acceptance of it.

The striking feature of Tocqueville's analysis of the Revolution is the continuity which he found between the old monarchy and the Revolutionary governments. The history of the monarchy was the record of a long and steady progress towards centralized absolutism. The monarchy itself had destroyed most of the elements of feudalism and most of the diverse restraints on its own power. The Revolution merely continued this development and even borrowed from its predecessor such instruments as the *intendant*. It wiped out the remnants of feudalism and achieved complete centralization. Even its equality was primarily equality before the law, and the old monarchy had been slowly establishing that. The Revolution, when it had completed the work of the monarchy, wielded such a centralized and unqualified authority that it was no more a regime of liberty than the rule of the Bourbons had been. The critics of the Revolution who assert that it was a sudden upheaval which instituted a tyranny in France are therefore mistaken, for the Revolution was not an innovation. But those who defend the Revolution as the source of liberty are mistaken, too, for the centralized and absolute power exercised by both the monarchy and the Revolution are the negation of liberty.

Edgar Quinet's *La Révolution,* published in 1865, revealed, in a different form, a similar reaction to the victory of the Second Empire over the Republic.[13] Quinet (1803–1875) was a man of letters and a professor, well known as a friend of Michelet, a republican, and an enemy of the Church, especially of the Ultramontanists. He presented his history of the Revolution as the work of a republican and a supporter of the principles of the Revolution. But, as a defender of the Revolution, he denounced the influence of the Jacobins and the policies associated with the Terror. Earlier historians who sympathized with the Revolution had not ordinarily identified themselves with the policies of the Terror, but they had directed attention to the causes which induced it and to the benefits which had come in spite of it. Quinet, however, attacked the Terror as the negation of the Revolution by the revolutionaries. His account is further distinguished for the fashion in which he criticized Revolutionary policy towards the Church. The Revolution did wrong in curbing the Church without destroying it; it should have supplanted Catholicism with Protestantism as a form of Christianity more sympathetic to liberty.

The scant dozen studies of the Revolution which have been considered briefly here constitute the outstanding works of the half-century preceding the Third Republic. They do not represent the sum of historical research on the Revolution during this period, nor are all of them distinguished from their contemporaries by superior scholarship. But they are the accounts which received widest attention in their day and which carried over into the Third Republic as the foremost thought of earlier generations on the interpretation of Revolutionary history.

A broad correspondence is immediately apparent between Revolutionary historiography and contemporary politics during these years. The support which developed during the Restoration for the establishment of a constitutional monarchy was furthered by a school of historians, of whom Mignet was perhaps the most notable, that presented the Revolution as an essentially sound movement which became pernicious when the monarch failed to concede a real representative government. The cause of republicanism, which gained ground under the Orleans monarchy, was likewise justified in the historiography of the Revolution, and the historians who are grouped about Michelet and Louis Blanc found the Republic a proper outcome of the Revolution, even though they were distressed by the violence which accompanied it. The disillusionment with the Revolution which developed to some extent with the establishment of the Second Empire likewise coincided with a more severe criticism of Revolutionary history.

The historical judgments on the Revolution presented before 1871 are further noteworthy for the differences they reveal when compared to those which came later. The array of diverging interpretations shifted significantly with the establishment of the Third Republic. The histories which had gained most prominence in the earlier period had generally favored the cause of the Revolution. The chief division was between constitutional monarchists and republicans; no work which entirely rejected the Revolution had received attention comparable to that granted theirs. But the tendencies which dominated historical interpretation during the Third Republic were quite different. Taine's study of the Revolution soon established a strong current of opinion opposing the whole Revolutionary movement (though not all its results) which persists to the present day. The republican tradition of Revolutionary history, begun early in the century, continued under the Third Republic and, in a new form, achieved an official position. But the school of historians which defended the Revolution yet qualified its support by argument for a constitutional monarchy lost all its vitality after 1871 and produced no new work of importance. The conservative and republican historians shared the whole field until the firm establishment of a socialist interpretation in the twentieth century forced a new alignment.

CHAPTER THREE

DURING THE STRUGGLE ABOUT THE REPUBLIC

THE EVENTS of 1870–1871 which brought the Second Empire to an end and created the situation from which the Third Republic emerged presented France with another of its nineteenth-century crises, but did not sharply break the continuity of French social history.[1] The course initiated by the National Assembly, which took over full exercise of the state power early in 1871, reveals acute controversy over the form of government and stable agreement on its underlying social bases, the same compound that had been the pattern of French history since early in the century.

The National Assembly dealt readily with most of the immediate problems it inherited from the Empire.[2] Peace was quickly made with the victorious Germans. A few policies which had been closely associated with the Empire came to an end: these included tariff liberalism and French support for the temporal power of the Papacy. Some changes were made in the personnel of the government, but the greater part of the administrative posts long continued to be filled by the same functionaries as under the Empire. The alteration in the diplomatic position of France which followed from the military defeat, and the humiliating effect of this on the French national spirit lay beyond the power of the Assembly to affect largely.

The constitutional crisis left by the fall of the Empire was not settled by the National Assembly, however. A struggle over the form of government dominated the foreground of French public life for more than twenty years, from 1871 until into the 1890s, and it never within the life of the Third Republic ceased to be an acute problem.

The Bonapartists played no important part in this conflict: their defeat proved to be decisive. A small group remained faithful to the Bonapartist cause and had some influence on the development of affairs, notably when they merged into the Boulangist agitation. But they were unable to take effective measures in furtherance of their own cause, and when they eventually suffered the embarrassment of rival claimants to the succession, they ceased to form a considerable independent force.

The overwhelming majority of the National Assembly was made up of monarchists, who seemed to have an excellent opportunity to restore the throne. But the cause of monarchy still suffered from the split between Legitimists and Orleanists, each of whom controlled about one third of the votes in the Assembly. Under the urgent pressure of their joint opportunity, the two groups strove towards reconciliation, and in 1873 they completed arrangements to enthrone the Comte de Chambord, the Legitimist claimant. At the last moment, however, his intransigent insistence on Legitimist principles caused the plans to miscarry, and the restoration was not accomplished. The breach thus reopened was not closed again until after the royalists had lost their position of power.

The republicans, ultimately the victors in the long constitutional crisis, won their success in the face of serious disadvantages. They had taken power directly after the abdication of Louis-Napoléon at Sedan. This doubtful privilege had been readily granted them by the royalists, who were not anxious to assume responsibility for the conduct of a war which was fast being lost. In the elections to the National Assembly, the republicans received only a third of the seats. Then the republican forces suffered severely from the insurrection of the Paris Commune during the next few months. The National Assembly decisively crushed the Commune and, with it, a strong republican faction. Although the republican groups in the Assembly disavowed the Commune and shared in the repression, they were discredited with the conservative classes, who again linked the cause of the Republic with that of social disorder.

The royalists proved less able to overcome their disadvantages than the republicans, and they were forced with great reluctance to establish the Republic. The Republic proclaimed by the provisional Government of National Defense had been continued by the National Assembly only as a temporary device until the peace treaty should be concluded and the split in the royalist forces mended. But when efforts at the restoration of monarchy failed in 1872 and 1873 and there seemed no further immediate likelihood of success, the Republic was supplied with constitutional laws of such sort as to facilitate a monarchist restoration in the near future.

The Republic so conditionally established was subjected to repeated attacks in the succeeding decades. The continuation of republican government tended to give the Republic the security of an established regime and enable it to moblize the popular support which was becoming increasingly evident. So, within two years after the passage of the constitutional laws of 1875, the royalists attempted to counter the growing strength of republicanism and embarked on the campaign of the *Seize-mai*.[3] A general election was forced in 1876-1877 about the issue of the form of government. While the royalists were even weaker and more divided then than they had been during the National Assembly, the republicans had gained strength and achieved a real electoral unity, and they emerged from the campaign in an even stronger position.

The controversy about the form of government then subsided for about ten years, until it burst forth again in the agitation centering in General Boulanger.[4] The Boulangist threat to the Republic was much stronger than that of the *Seize-mai*, since Boulanger had a real popular following as well as the secret assistance of powerful royalist forces. But the Boulangists, for all their criticism of the parliamentary regime of the Republic, had no alternative program and scarcely any suggestions for one. This violent agitation against the Republic came to a bankrupt end when General Boulanger, after gaining sufficient strength to overthrow the Republic, refused to do so.

The resistance of the right to the Republic remained strong enough in the last decade of the century to make the republican form of government a central issue in the Dreyfus affair.[5] But the opposition was by then so disorganized that the only overt actions which might have threatened the government were of less than comic-opera stature.

The struggle to establish the republican form of government thus continually occupied the center of French political life for more than twenty years.

But, for all its prominence, this conflict was confined to narrow limits. The parties which waged this unrelenting fight were in substantial agreement on most questions of political and social institutions.

All important parties, regardless of their relation to republicanism, granted the essentials of political liberalism. There was no dispute over the political rights of citizens, a wide or universal suffrage, and parliamentary government through a ministry responsible to the legislature. The creation of the Senate aroused considerable criticism, to be sure, but the movement to revise the constitution in this respect lost support the closer the issue came to a decision. The Boulangist agitation expressed in some measure a reaction against parliamentary government, but its force was checked by the almost complete lack of an alternative proposal. Although there were elements on the right and the left which repudiated the demands of liberalism or qualified their support of them, none of the parties of influence, from Legitimists to extreme left, stood full against the current.

The general acceptance of liberalism was complemented by a rejection of the kind of democracy in which the common people themselves would actually exercise political power. The fate of the Paris Commune of 1871 had demonstrated that.[6] The insurrection of Paris was the result of varied influences and the expression of contradictory aspirations. But the aim which underlay all others and in which all groups within the Commune shared was the creation of a popular democracy. The government of the National Assembly crushed the insurrection so ruthlessly and thoroughly as to ensure that such an effort would not be repeated for generations to come. The Assembly approved the repression with scarcely a dissenting vote. So decisive was the repudiation of the Commune by the parliamentary parties that even Gambetta, who led the republican left, refused as late as 1880 to support the demand for a general amnesty for those who had taken part in the uprising.

The relationship of state to society also lay outside the area of political conflict. The balance of forces between the capitalist middle class and the land-owning aristocracy, which had been struck early in the century, persisted into the Third Republic. The transition from Empire to Republic brought no change in the prevailing economic system. The Paris Commune bore an element of challenge to the working of capitalism, but certainly not through the conscious intent of the majority of its supporters. Even the question of the proper sphere of state intervention in economic life, sharply debated during these years in every country where the influence of the Manchester school had penetrated, produced little controversy in France. There were doctrinaire liberals, of course, but questions of state policy were not determined by them.

The long struggle about the Republic was not meaningless, however, even though it did not penetrate deeply into the structure of government and society.

The right and the left saw eye to eye on the need for particular institutions, but they attached widely diverging purposes and values to them. The dominant elements in French public life largely agreed on immediate proposals, but they were divided in social philosophy. The underlying differences in social politics were expressed in support of the Republic, or opposition to it; and attitudes towards the Republic, in turn, were bound to evaluations of the heritage of the Great Revolution.

Conflicts on this level—the social philosophies conventionally expressed in terms of the significance of the Revolution—cut through the general agreement on points of immediate practical importance. This circumstance produced both the recurring crises over republican government and the otherwise stable development of French public life during these years.

The grave importance attached to the social philosophy behind a working agreement was strikingly illustrated in the course of the attempted monarchist restoration of 1873.[7] The Orleanist and Legitimist deputies in the National Assembly, both conscious of the need to settle their differences as soon as possible and to take advantage of the opportunity to effect a restoration, had largely succeeded in drawing up a mutually acceptable arrangement. The constitutional proposals offered by the Orleanists were agreeable to the Legitimists. The Orleanists were content to enthrone the Legitimist claimant, the Comte de Chambord, with the understanding that since he had no direct heir, the Orleanist pretender, the Comte de Paris, would succeed him. In the course of conferences between the Comte de Chambord and Charles Chesnelong, an Orleanist deputy who undertook to negotiate with him, the Comte de Chambord indicated that he approved the arrangements, even on the point which he had made the symbol of his cause: he would give up his insistence on the adoption of the white banner of the Bourbons as the national flag rather than the tricolor. There was no apparent reason why the restoration should not be consummated.

But the Comte de Chambord, on reflection, felt that the spirit in which he viewed these practical proposals might be misunderstood. His honor obliged him to make his attitude unmistakable. Even as the plans for the restoration were being completed, he issued a public statement which concluded with these words: "Never will I consent to become the legitimate King of the Revolution." Such a simple reference to the Revolution was enough to identify the social philosophy which he repudiated. The Orleanists and other parties attached quite as much importance to this expression of the spirit behind the practical accord as the Comte de Chambord did, and the working agreement was shattered. The attempt at restoration was laid aside and royalist hopes received an almost mortal blow.

The diverging social philosophies which gave rise to the struggle for and against the Republic were fundamentally conditioned by the modes of life of the social groups which were aligned behind one or another ideology. But the expression of these contrary views was so intimately associated with evaluations of the Great Revolution that they can not be properly understood apart from the historical judgments which they embraced. The historical interpretations of the Revolution must therefore be considered first, then the social forces which lay behind them.

The defeat of 1870–1871, the outburst of the Paris Commune, and the prolonged constitutional crisis which followed on the destruction of the Second Empire turned much of the attention of France to the problem of the proper basis of national life in the effort to find a way by which France might escape from its national humiliation and its political instability.

It was natural, therefore, that such a prominent intellectual figure as H. A. Taine should turn to this problem during the early 1870s. Taine (1828–1893) had established his pre-eminence in French intellectual life during the Empire. His writings on literature, philosophy, art, and history had secured him an international audience. He had strongly influenced the course of French criticism in the direction of determinism, materialism, and the imitation of science. The weight of his writings had been so great that when he and Renan both became candidates for academic positions in 1863, the Archbishop of Paris, Mgr Dupanloup, had made their candidacies the occasion for a sharp attack on the tendencies which each represented.

It was in the French Revolution that Taine sought the roots of the political situation of the France in which he was living. His intention was to write a series of books under the general title of *Les Origines de la France contemporaine*. He published one volume on *L'Ancien Régime* in 1875,[8] and three volumes on *La Révolution* between 1878 and 1884.[9] But his work on *Le Régime moderne,* of which two volumes appeared, he was unable to bring to a finished form before his death in 1893.

The study which Taine presented of the *ancien régime* showed a distant sympathy for it but by no means underwrote its cause.

The old order was not without its virtues, but by 1789 it had outlived its usefulness and could no longer have been kept alive. The aristocracy of France had once justified the privileges with which it was endowed by rendering a service to society in protecting it from disorder. But this historic condition no longer obtained.[10] The central government had taken over the local functions of the nobles and had reduced their duties to the services of courtiers. The privileges of the king himself were diverted from the use of France to that of the court. The court nobility did develop a salon culture of much charm and admirable polish, remarkable for the high responsibility of the individual to the social group in which he lived.[11] But the virtues of this society produced matching defects: an artificial sensitivity coupled with aridity, and insufficiency of character.

The ultimate condemnation of the way of life of the aristocrats was that they lost their ability to fight for survival: "As they acquired talents suited to calm times, they lost those which are suited to troublous times; extreme weakness overcame them at the very moment that they achieved the utmost urbanity. The more refined an aristocracy becomes, the weaker it grows, and when it succeeds at last in perfecting a charming manner, it entirely loses its strength. And yet, in this world, one must struggle if one wants to live. The right to rule depends on the power to rule, with mankind as with nature."[12]

In the midst of this gracious but enervated society, the force was developed which was to destroy it: the revolutionary spirit. This was a fusion of two elements within the civilization of the *ancien régime*: the accomplishments of science, and classicism. The dominance of classical standards in French intellectual life had put the mark of highest value on the universal and abstract; what was concrete and particular was considered of a lower order and lesser importance. The power of reason had been raised to a high position at the same time through the accomplishments of science. These two developments combined to produce a new kind of rationalism, one that was fully confident of its ability to remodel the world for the better and scorned the restraints of history and the peculiarities of concrete circumstances.[13]

This revolutionary spirit grew to threatening proportions as it came to be attached to the real grievances of the mass of the people, who suffered under the burden of the regime of privilege. The middle class had risen to a position of influence and ability but bore numerous unjustified disabilities.[14] The peasantry was in a truly miserable state, for the people of the countryside could barely keep themselves alive in good times, and whenever the harvest failed they were decimated.[15] In such a situation it was suicidal folly for the privileged classes to toy with the explosive revolutionary ideas.

Such an analysis of the *ancien régime* left a certain ambiguity as to Taine's view of the responsibility for the Revolution. While he disapproved of the principles of systematic reform, he presented them as a product of the old order itself and a condemnation of it, and he did not minimize the grievances of the French people. The book received wide attention, but it was not immediately apparent whether Taine was to be counted with the friends of the Revolution or its enemies. Taine made his position unmistakable at the outset of his next volume, and he took his place in the vanguard of the attack on the Revolution.

The storming of the Bastille revealed the true monarch of the Revolution: "the people, that is, *the mob,* a hundred, a thousand, ten thousand individuals fortuitously gathered together upon a motion or an alarm and transformed immediately and irresistibly into legislators, judges, and executioners. A formidable, destructive, and shapeless beast that can not be curbed, it sits at the portals of the Revolution together with its mother, the baying monster Liberty, like Milton's two specters at the gates of Hell."[16]

The men of the National Assembly bear a large responsibility for the vicious spread of the Revolution. Their intention was not evil, but they were so badly infected with the revolutionary disease that they were quite unable to check the destructive force of the insurrectionary mob. So a spontaneous anarchy held sway over France throughout their term of office. Their great fault was that instead of creating a strong government which would restore order they simply perpetuated the existing anarchy in the Constitution of 1791.

The rise of the Jacobin party was the event of overshadowing importance during the regime of the Legislative Assembly. The Jacobin party was not drawn from the old privileged classes, of course, save for a few individual renegades. Nor, generally, did the "men who held positions of authority in society, or deserved to, furnish recruits to the party. . . . Furthermore, the revolutionary theory did not receive even an audience in the great mass of the common people nor in the rural areas until after it had been transformed into a legend. . . . The theory gained its supporters elsewhere, between the two social extremes, in the lower ranks of the bourgeoisie and the upper ranks of the common people . . . [From these classes, it did not draw the substantial members, but only] a very small minority, a restless and innovating minority: for one part, those who were not firmly attached to their trades or professions because they held only secondary or subordinate positions . . . for the other part, men who were unstable in character, all those had been uprooted by the general upheaval."[17]

When the Jacobins had gained dominance within the Revolutionary forces, the movement swept past the modest bounds of the Legislative Assembly to reach its fullest extent in the Convention. The old privileged classes bear an indirect responsibility for the extension. Not that they provoked it by resistance to legitimate demands for reform. The nobility suffered patiently for more than thirty months before it began to give resistance to its persecutors.[18] The King himself was quite willing to live within the Constitution, confident that experience would teach the nation that more power must be granted to the executive.[19] But this very willingness of the aristocracy to cooperate with the representatives of the people strengthened the Jacobin cause. Only a strong government could protect the nation from the Jacobins, yet after July 14 there was no longer any effective government. France lay defenseless before the onslaught of the revolutionaries.[20]

As the Jacobins extended their power, their party was "purified," for the revolutionary forces underwent a process of selection which thrust the worst elements to the fore. Of the original revolutionary movement, about all that remained in 1793 were "unreliable workmen, vagabonds of town and country, inmates of almshouses, the riff-raff from low resorts, the degraded and dangerous populace, the outcasts from every class. At Paris, whence they issued commands to the rest of France, their gang was a minority of the smallest sort, recruited precisely from that human trash which infests capital cities, from the epileptic and scrofulous rabble, heirs of a corrupt blood further diluted by their own misconduct, who import into civilization the degeneracies, the imbecility, the defects of their broken-down constitutions, their retrogressive instincts, and their ill-formed heads."[21]

The Jacobin program set the regeneration of man as its goal. The requisite for this was the reduction of all distinctions among men, the destruction of the Church and the aristocracy, first that of birth and then that of wealth. To this end were sacrificed castes, churches, guilds, provinces, communes, families.[22]

The ultimate content of the Revolutionary idea, as it was revealed during the period of Jacobin power, is an attack on property: "Whatever the great names, Liberty, Equality, Fraternity, with which the Revolution decks itself out, it is, in essence, a *transfer of property;* in that consists its original source of strength, its power to endure, its inmost support, and its historic meaning."[23]

But the Jacobin republic could not last indefinitely nor even avert its own downfall, for its nature was such that it destroyed the necessary basis for any state, the mutual respect of its members. "When the Jacobin republic died, it was not only because it had grown decrepit and was killed; it was also because it had not been born viable: from its origin, it contained within itself a principle of dissolution, an inward and fatal poison, not only for others but for itself."[24]

The evil did not end with the fall of the Jacobins, however: it persisted through the Directory and long after. The Directory could not restore order nor even achieve stability within its own ranks. It was succeeded by a regime which united philosophy and a sword, and France became a "philosophic barracks."[25]

Taine's interpretation of the Revolution, as a whole, did not vindicate the *ancien régime* as against its successor. The old order had exhausted its historic justification. The governing class, become defenseless through its own refinement, itself fostered the revolutionary spirit which was to destroy it. The nation had real grievances against the government. So a legitimate task lay upon the Revolution: to remove the burden of outworn privileges from the nation and to place effective restraints on an absolute government which had become arbitrary. Concretely, this meant creating equality of citizens in respect to taxation and establishing control by representatives of the nation over public expenditure.[26] The proper function of government, as Taine viewed it, followed the classical liberal conception of the watchdog state: to maintain a diplomatic and military establishment and a system of law courts and police.[27]

But Taine's criticism of the Revolution did not argue so much for an alternative line of development as against the universal reforming tendency for which the Revolution was the starting point; his was a negative rather than an affirmative viewpoint. Taine condemned the Revolution as a continuous whole, a body of doctrines which, once granted, can not be modified short of their natural fulfillment. The Revolution purported to express the power of abstract reason to refashion human institutions for the better, without respecting tradition or the weight of concrete circumstances. It actually resulted in reducing all the mediating forces between the citizen and the state— family, church, social distinctions. Its ultimate outcome was an equalitarian attack on private property. Since no society can exist without private property and its accompanying institutions, the Revolution can be completed only when it totally destroys the basis for social order.

Taine's history of the Revolution immediately won itself rank as the classic conservative analysis. It sold widely at the time of publication and continued to have an active life for decades afterwards. No previous study of the Revolution of comparable stature had so bitterly challenged the whole Revolutionary movement. The interpretation left a deep imprint on the work of later conservatives and, by reaction, on the historical work of the left as well. The high esteem which the right gave to Taine's history marked a shift in Taine's position, for he had earlier been sharply assailed by strong conservative elements for the materialist and anti-religious tendency of his writings.

The place accorded Taine as an opponent of the Revolution rested on a sound base, however, for the tendency of his interpretation fitted well with the general social philosophy of the right in the 1870s and 1880s.[28]

The forces of which the right was composed had drawn together well before the Third Republic. Its core was made up of the royalist families of the landed aristocracy. Many of these were descended, more or less directly, from the nobility of the *ancien régime*. But a large number had been added by the successive regimes of the nineteenth century, as middle-class families amassed wealth, bought provincial estates, and obtained aristocratic rank in one fashion or another. The ideology of the royalists had a similarly mixed derivation, partly from the old order and partly from nineteenth-century sources. It rested on the defense of tradition and stability and support for the throne and the Church. The eighteenth-century justification of monarchical society had been transformed by the events of the Revolutionary epoch and, since the Restoration, showed the diverse influence of religious, romantic, liberal, and authoritarian tendencies. But the landed aristocracy continued to defend a stable hierarchy of social status as natural, proper, inevitable.

This sort of conservatism came readily to the families of the countryside, for it conformed to their way of life. The fall of the Versailles monarchy destroyed the domination which the Court and courtier life held over the nobility, and the aristocracy of the nineteenth century lived more commonly on their provincial estates. In the provinces, generation succeeded generation without witnessing startling change: the rhythm of life varied little with the passing of years. In the lands of their estates, the noble families held positions of respect and authority in a social hierarchy, and the peasant population of the outlying regions remained under the influence of the manorial family. The older aristocrats would occasionally, during the early years of the Third Republic, deplore the decline of *bonnetage*—the peasants were no longer careful to doff their caps to their natural superiors. That this complaint should be made indicates the deference which was still customarily expected of the country people.

Royalism had long since adjusted itself to the requirements of the business life of the cities, however, and was not confined to the families of landed wealth and their retainers. The Orleanists had readily adapted themselves to the interests of the middle class, but the Legitimists as well assented to the fundamental demands of capitalist development. The right offered no important resistance to the operation of bourgeois economic life. Indeed, capitalism, as well as capitalists, was admitted even to the estates of the countryside. The adjustment of royalism to the political demands of the middle class was as real, though less perfect. By the time of the Third Republic, both Legitimists and Orleanists had accepted most of the institutions of political liberalism.

As the royalists made this adjustment to the middle class, the bourgeoisie was forced towards the right by fear of the further revolutionary implications of republicanism. The middle-class revolutions of the early century had drawn in their wake a popular movement of growing dimensions. The main objectives of the democratic revolutionaries had been political and centered in the Republic, but they were commonly associated with aspirations towards social democracy. The element that was consciously socialist was small, its principles were not defined in clear and commonly shared terms, and it was supported only by part of the petty bourgeoisie and an infant proletariat. But this extreme left was a source of deep distrust to the more powerful bourgeois and had been struck down severely, but with increasing difficulty, in 1830, 1848, and 1871. The fears aroused by the Paris Commune, especially, remained alive into the 1880s.

The opposition of the right to systematic reform of a socializing tendency and its unequivocal defense of property served to attract the support of substantial sections of the middle class. The royalist right was not without social conscience, to be sure: there was a tradition of humanitarian patronage among the old nobility, based on Christian charity. The Comte de Mun was able to draw on this resource in building the Social Catholic movement. But the right as a whole could be counted on for defense of property and for resistance to change in the social order.

Support for royalism from within the upper bourgeoisie was further facilitated by the fact that the mode of life of many middle-class families was not unlike that of the families of landed wealth. The development of business life in France remained comparatively slow throughout most of the nineteenth century: the quick change characteristic of the industrial revolution was not accented until the closing decade. During the earlier years commercial or banking families were not uncommon; in them, wealth and a way of living firmly ordered by unchanging conventions passed from one generation to another. The sense of stability, hierarchy, and social order was as natural to such middle-class families as to those of the nobility who lived on their estates.

The political career of the right during the early years of the Third Republic reflected the nature of the forces which entered into its composition. The conservatives were most concerned during this period with halting that tendency towards dangerous and unsettling social reform which had its origin in the Revolution and its contemporary expression in republicanism. They did not propose to undo the Revolution: they conceded almost all the specific political demands which were urged in the name of the Revolution. But they were gravely alarmed at the use which the republicans were making of the Revolutionary tradition to spread a movement of systematic reform. The republicans were thereby undermining the general respect for social hierarchy, sapping the authority of the Church, and threatening to destroy all the bulwarks of social order.

The ineffectual but bitter struggle which the right waged against the Republic arose from this situation. Because the conservatives conceded so much of republican institutions, they could not offer a really alternative form of government; and because they were striving to check the Revolutionary spirit, they would not accept the Republic in which that spirit was embodied.

The interpretation of the Revolution which Taine offered in the early years of the Third Republic corresponded largely with the viewpoint of the conservatives who so readily endorsed his work.

Taine considered that the *ancien régime* had outlived its historic justification, yet violently condemned the Revolutionary movement which destroyed it. The right similarly struggled unrelentingly against republicanism, but did not propose, any more than Taine, that the conditions of the pre-Revolutionary order should be restored. Quite like Taine, the right accepted the fundamental achievements of the Revolution as legitimate and permanent. These included the juridical equality of citizens and the establishment of representative government.

Taine vigorously opposed the Revolutionary movement, but did not attack the middle class which had played so large a part in it. The right, in contemporary politics, similarly resisted the middle-class republican movement, but clearly did not represent a force opposed to the middle class. Nor did Taine charge the Revolution against the common people of France. It was rather the work of a small minority of *déclassés,* organized by political bandit-chiefs. Such a view could readily be approved by the men of the right, for they themselves sought to repress only those elements among the common people who resisted their subordination.

The element which Taine made the center of his analysis of the — Revolution was the very one that defined the position of the right which made him its historian: the attack on the spirit of the Revolution. It is this which links the two. Taine saw the prime source of the Revolution, not in the conditions of the old order which demanded change, nor in the development of new classes to positions of power, but in the spirit of abstract and rationalist reform directed at a refashioning of society, in disregard of tradition or the special characteristics of a particular situation. Once the principles of the Revolution are conceded, there is no place at which to call a halt until all traditional institutions—the Church, the family, social distinctions, private property—are destroyed in favor of uniformity and equality. This is nothing less than the end of society itself.

Such an interpretation gave articulate expression, in the history of the Revolution, to the social views which the right was urging in the early years of the Third Republic.

The appearance of Taine's study in the early years of the Third Republic marked a sharp change in historical judgment of the Revolution. The histories which had attained greatest renown in the preceding fifty years had generally supported the cause of the Revolution and were divided chiefly between constitutional-monarchist and republican sympathies. The tendency of opinion which entirely opposed the Revolutionary movement had not received an expression of comparable authority until Taine's treatment. The defense of the Revolution after Taine's time became the charge of the republicans: the position of the constitutional monarchists had lost its vitality.

The republican analysis of the Revolution, which confronted the conservative and supplied part of its meaning, did not produce any single work during the years in which Taine was publishing which corresponded to his in dimensions and stature. Michelet's history continued to pass as the classic republican interpretation and it was not displaced before the turn of the century.

Fresh writing of considerable influence was being offered by republican historians during these early years, however, and formed a clearly defined body of opinion. This may be called the Opportunist school, for it was developed by men who were closely associated with Gambetta and the Opportunist republicans and parallelled their viewpoint on contemporary political issues.

The newspaper *La République française,* the organ of Gambetta and the Opportunists, consistently encouraged historical writings in defense of the Revolution and published monographs and reviews on the subject in its pages. Three men who were closely associated with Gambetta frequently submitted such material. Georges Avenel (1828–1876) had worked with Gambetta in the republican opposition under the Empire. He became one of the editors of *La République française* at its founding in 1871 and conducted a regular feature in it entitled *Lundis révolutionnaires.* Here he criticized current work on the Revolution from his own large knowledge of the literature of the subject. Marcellin Pellet (b. 1849) pursued a modest career as an Opportunist deputy from 1876 to 1885. Eugène Spuller (1835–1896), also an Opportunist deputy, was a figure of more prominence. He became a chief leader of the Opportunists after Gambetta's death and held ministerial positions of some importance. The articles on the history of the Revolution which each of these men contributed to *La République française* in the early years of the Republic were later published in book form.[29] From these collections, the republican interpretation of the Revolution during these years may be illustrated.

The historians of the left challenged Taine's analysis at the very point which he had selected as the true source of the Revolution: the revolutionary spirit. The core of the Revolution, in the conservative view, was the determination of a small group of men to put certain ideas into action. But, for the republicans, the Revolution did not spring from the minds of the revolutionaries, whether their ideas were good or bad, but from the circumstances of the old order, from the inefficiency and injustice of the absolute monarchy.

That the Revolution did not arise from the currency of anti-monarchical ideas is strikingly evidenced by the fact that there was not a single expression of republicanism in 1789,[30] only three years before the Revolution was to find its natural culmination in the Republic. Far from harboring an intention to overturn the throne, France was entirely loyal to the monarchy and simply sought relief for certain grievances. Only as the resistance of the privileged classes demonstrated that these legitimate reforms could not be accomplished under the monarchy did the nation turn to the Republic.

The development of the Revolution from the Estates to the Convention was governed throughout by circumstances, as France learned from its experience. The declaration of war by the Legislative Assembly was one of the capital decisions in this forward progress of the Revolution. The war was a recognition of the solidarity and resistance of the old order. It was provoked by the hostility of the monarchist coalition, which feared the spread of the reform movement and hoped to seize an opportunity to gratify its ambitions against France. The Revolutionary war became a great national effort and, at the same time, a work of liberation.[31]

The Convention itself was likewise controlled by the requirements of the situation in which it found itself. "Is there need, at this date, to debate about the period of the Convention? Must it be demonstrated that, if the new Assembly no longer had to fear Louis XVI, it was in no less danger from executive powers of an entirely different sort, the generals, and that all the efforts of Paris were directed to protecting the Assembly from the influence and the force of the military? Was it the Commune or Dumouriez who spoke of marching against the judges of Louis XVI, the representatives of the people?"[32]

When the Mountain drove the Girondists from the Convention and assumed control, it was not for theoretical reasons but in response to the very real fact that the Gironde was in contact with the enemy. Under the leadership of the Mountain, the Convention brought the Revolution to its highest point.

The republican historians did not agree precisely on the character of the different groups within the Mountain, nor on the forces governing the development of the Terror. But they all treated the period as one of a striving for freedom and equality, defined in political terms. The Directory, which succeeded the Convention, they all disowned, for its incompetence led to the capture of France by the Bonapartist dictatorship.[33]

Although the republican historians denied that Revolutionary rationalism had caused the upheaval of 1789, they did not deprecate the value of the ideas which the Revolution expressed. They presented these principles, indeed, as the great legacy of the Revolution. Spuller, for example, declared that "The French Revolution had its basic and true cause in the higher conception of law. The French people believed with a profound faith and a generous heart in the definitive advent of justice, and determined to bring it about. The Revolution is to be found there; to look for it elsewhere is to misunderstand and underestimate it."[34] In contrast to the conservative interpretation, the republicans emphasized the circumstances of the times rather than the ideas of the revolutionaries as the source of the Revolution. But the circumstances which determined the course of the Revolution were not simply the interests and demands of certain classes in France; they were concrete contradictions of the eternal principles of justice and liberty.

The Liberty, Equality, and Fraternity of the Revolution, in the view of the Opportunist historians, did not entail social equality. Avenel, for example, replied to a German critic who had charged that the Revolution fostered communism, that there was no evidence to this effect, and, indeed, that it was the Germans who had the baneful primacy with respect to communist ideas.[35] In answer to the socialists who were asserting that the proletarian Fourth Estate had yet to make its own revolution, because that of the bourgeois Third was insufficient, Spuller directly denied the reality of the Fourth Estate: the Third Estate was not a class, but the nation.[36]

In the struggle between the Revolution and the privileged Church, the republican historians took their stand with the revolutionaries. The first breach between the Church and the Revolution was created by the resistance of the Church to the necessary measures of reform taken by the revolutionary party.[37] But beneath the issue of property rights of the Church lay a profound antagonism between the spirit of the ancient Church and that of the modern society which the Revolution was founding. It was the historic duty of the Revolution to forward that struggle in the interest of progress and to free the nation of the reactionary restraints which the Church wished to impose on it.[38]

That this interpretation of the Revolution formed an integral part of the contemporary politics of the left, the authors made quite clear and explicit.[39]

The republican left of this generation was entirely controlled by middle-class leaders. The republican movement had always been supported by some sections of the middle class, although the fear that the Republic would lead to social disorder had alienated the upper bourgeoisie. The insurrection of the Paris Commune had renewed this association of social upheaval with the Republic, but the conservative Republic of Thiers had struck down the Commune, the parliamentary republicans had disavowed it, and the passage of time showed that the Republic need not lead to social revolution. So conservative elements of the middle class came in increasing numbers in the 1870s and 1880s to accept the Third Republic. The republican left never secured the allegiance of the whole middle class, however; some portions remained in opposition or shifted from one side of the center to the other.

The republican left drew a large part of its strength from the work-ing class in the cities and from the country people in many regions. The independent participation of the working class in political life had been destroyed in the repression of the Paris Commune and did not resume until the emergence of the socialist movement in the 1890s; but in the meantime, the republicans were able to count on its support. General Boulanger was able to capitalize for a time on a popular disillusion-ment with the Republic, but the Boulangists were able to threaten the Republic only under a public character of ultrarepublicanism. Steady and increasing popular support was largely responsible for the survival of the Third Republic during its perilous first two or three decades.

The left was democratic as well as republican. It fought for all the liberal conventions by which the whole people were formally ad-mitted to the exercise of sovereignty. But it would not tolerate the actual entrance of the common people into government, as its share in the repression of the Commune demonstrated. The republican left, indeed, took over none of the tradition of the Commune: that was left to the later socialists. It shared in the democratic nationalism that was so much a mark of the Commune, but it had a good claim to nationalism in its own right. The Gambetta left, in fine, fought for the political rights of the people with the confident presumption that the power of the people would actually be directed by members of the middle class for purposes of their choosing.

The program of the left held only a slight social content during this generation. So far as the middle class was concerned its major social demands were conceded by all parties and were not the special business of the republicans. For the condition of the common people, the republicans troubled little. Gambetta declared that there was no social problem, there were only social problems. But even with an empirical formulation, the republicans showed small interest in re-dressing social disparities or relieving social distress. They did not make an issue of state intervention in behalf of labor: the few modest labor laws which were passed during this period did not occasion even second-rank party conflicts. A demand for a progressive income tax had, to be sure, formed part of the program of the extreme left since the last years of the Empire. But the income tax remained only an item in electoral manifestoes until a later generation.

The long struggle which the republicans waged against the right did not spring, it is evident, from a sharp differentiation of the forces which made up each group, nor from contradictory programs. The republican right was controlled by members of the middle class, although it also drew support from the workingmen and peasants. The right, although it was primarily associated with the landed aristocracy, was fully adjusted to the requirements of the middle class and drew large support from it. The left was so little separated from the right in respect to the form of government that the constitution drawn up by the royalists was never revised, save in a small detail, when the republicans came to power.

It was their defense of a system of ideas derived from the Revolution that most clearly divided the republicans from the right. By invoking the principles of the Revolution, the republicans justified popular sovereignty and the formal equality expressed in the democratic republic and extolled the French nation. The right insisted that such principles opened the way for an attack by the masses on the foundations of the social order. But the republicans were fully confident that if the common people were admitted to the exercise of state power and were made conscious of the common interests of the nation, they could be so guided that there would be no disturbance of the proper basis of society.

As they were translated into political action, these republican principles centered in a vigorous anticlericalism. The struggle against the influence of the Church played a part of great importance in the republican politics. It was the point at which the left was best able to distinguish itself from the right, with which it agreed on so many other problems. This issue served at the same time to draw the working class into alliance with the bourgeois republicans and to retard the organization of labor about the points where its interests conflicted with those of the middle class. The republicans were quite aware, too, that the political influence of the Church had given

strength to those elements of the right that had most strenuously resisted middle-class republicanism. So the left displayed an unflagging
energy in the effort to reduce the power of the Church. The republicans made anticlericalism a focus of their attention as they fought to
gain control of the newly established Republic. When they at last
won the seats of power during the 1880s, they turned directly to the
enactment of laic laws. Their answer to the protest which the right
raised against the Republic during the Dreyfus affair was again directed to the relations of Church and state and resulted in the termination of the Concordat.

The social politics of the republican left and the analysis of the Revolution which they endorsed thus interpenetrated deeply.

The Opportunist republicans presented their program as the contemporary fulfillment of the ideas of Liberty, Equality, and Fraternity
which the French nation had elaborated in the course of its struggle
to rectify the abuses of the *ancien régime*. These Revolutionary principles found their full expression, in contemporary France as in the
eighteenth century, only through the democratic republic, political and legal equality, the elevation of the people and the nation to
governing power.

This popular sovereignty was presumed to operate under the direction of the middle class, in the Third Republic as in the Revolution.
Revolutionary and republican equality was defined as the equality
of the ballot and the market place. The Revolution did not imply that
workingmen and peasants were themselves to direct the state: the
bourgeoisie acted as agents for the whole people. The Revolution
endorsed, rather than impugned, the relationship of employer and
worker.

All this did not mean, however, that there was a distinction between
the interests of the bourgeoisie and of the nation. The circumstances
of the old order had been such that the bourgeoisie was especially
ready to discover how national life must be ordered so as to conform
to the principles of Liberty, Equality, and Fraternity. But the republic
which the bourgeoisie founded was not the instrument of their special
interest: the middle class was not distinct from the nation.

The Revolution meant, finally, a smaller place for religion in — society. It implied, at least, that the state should no longer use its power to support the influence of the Church over the nation. The task of the Revolution, at any event, established a set of values other than those which the Church offered: the values which the republicans derived from the Revolution could be expressed in secular terms and largely satisfied in the course of day-to-day life in the world of affairs.

The two positions held by Taine and the Opportunist school represented the basic forms within which the Revolution was criticized by historians during the generation in which the Republic was founded. The writing of history was not a narrowly restricted profession during this age, and many writers who claimed no more than a general familiarity with the literature on the Revolution did not hesitate to publish their views on the subject. Most of the other general histories of the Revolution that appeared in these years followed the pattern of either Taine or the Opportunist school, without achieving a like authority.[40] The most significant contributions to the study of the Revolution came from the continuing monographic research, rather than from works so largely derivative.

An interpretive study of real substance and considerable freshness did appear towards the end of this period with the publication of Albert Sorel's work on the Revolution in its relations with the Europe of the old order.[41] Sorel (1842–1906) enjoyed an advantageous opportunity for research on the Revolution. The positions which he held as an official in the Ministry of Foreign Affairs from 1866 to 1876 and as secretary to the president of the Senate thereafter gave him ready access to materials in government archives. He was thus enabled to utilize much fresh material on the diplomatic history of the Revolution.

Sorel's treatment of the sources of the Revolution emphasized especially the conditions of the *ancien régime* in 1789. He acknowledged the spreading influence of the revolutionary spirit, but minimized its determining role in action. "The Revolution, imminent in almost all Europe, broke out in France because the old regime was further developed there and, at the same time, more insupportable, more abhorred and easier to destroy than elsewhere; because the government had created a need for reforms which it could not effect; because the state power, unable to direct opinion, no longer had the force to repress it; because the collapse of authority was accompanied by financial bankruptcy; because change seemed inevitable and every approach lay open to the innovators; and because, finally, all the doctrines of philosophy, which were more popular there than in any other country, had penetrated further into the nation and better suited its genius. It was that genius which impressed so individual a character on the French Revolution; this character remains essentially constant throughout the history of France. The classic spirit, which directed the Revolution, and the absolute government, which furnished the occasion for it, combined its elements, and determined its framework, were developed in France along parallel courses; they resulted from the same conception of man, society, state, philosophy, and art."[42]

The revolutionaries were absorbed with principles, metaphysics, deductions, only when they were holding discussions; when they faced the responsibility of action, they turned for guidance to the reality of French history. The philosophy of the Revolution interested only a small circle; the mass of the nation was not versed in its doctrines. "It saw in the Revolution a very practical and very real business, the abolition of the feudal regime, which was indeed its root. It saw in the armed emigration what was its real root, too—an attempt to re-establish the detested regime by force."[43] The fact is unquestionable that France gave no credence to republican ideas until after the Revolution was well under way.[44]

The constructive work of the Revolution proceeded through the first two assemblies to a peak in the Convention. At its highest point, "the Convention saved the national independence and unity of France and established civil liberty, the essential conquest of the Revolution; the equality that the French held dear; the sovereignty of the people, foundation of democracy, and law of the future. . . . In imitation of all earlier and contemporary governments, it confiscated the goods of defeated or proscribed adversaries of the state; but it transformed that violent act of public safety into a political operation which singularly modified its character and distinguished it from analogous measures taken by Louis XVI . . . [and other monarchs]. The Convention did not confiscate property in order to enrich the state, or to give endowments to its favorites or, by force alone, to put conquerors in the places of the conquered. . . . By that immense diffusion of property, the Convention consummated a revolution made for the liberation of persons and property. It linked these reforms to the idea of the fatherland: it made that great ideal a real part of the life of every Frenchman by binding his pride, his fortune, his dignity, and his virtues to the idea of patriotism."[45]

The Revolution turned off from its true course when it undertook a foreign war and fixed the conquest of natural frontiers as its stopping point.[46] This obliged the Revolution to wage war for an indefinite length of time. As Louis XIV had discovered, the other nations in Europe would not acquiesce in the conquest of natural limits so long as they could resist. The conditions imposed by such a war made it possible for the terrorists to "usurp the Republic under the pretext of defending it, and the noblest of causes served as a cloak for the most execrable of tyrannies."[47]

The Jacobins who thus seized control of the Revolution were the servants of masters even baser than themselves. "While the Jacobin chiefs led the Assembly and France, they themselves took their orders from the chiefs of the Parisian demagogy, and these demagogues represented only the army and the rebellious mob which followed them. If the Jacobins were the only organized body in France, the army was the only effective force. Without the army, the political parties could do nothing. They were, in reality, the clients of the obscure and uncouth anarchists who commanded it. . . . Paris abounded with unemployed workers, vagabonds, discharged soldiers, refugees from every quarter, a combination of hungry men, adventurers, and bandits, who were only awaiting an opportunity to move into action. To that horde of overwrought rogues to whom pillage had been promised was joined the fanatical troop of wretches to whom happiness had been assured; to those who wanted to sack France in order to share in the booty were added those who sought to destroy it for the sake of rebuilding it."[48]

The Terror contributed nothing to the successes of the armies at the front; the victories were won in spite of the Terror. Its only function was to maintain the terrorists in power.[49] Such a tyranny did not have an enduring base, and when internal rivalries among the terrorists produced the Thermidorean crisis, the nation was able to assert itself even against the faction which had overthrown Robespierre.[50]

The Directory, which succeeded the Terror, was not able to resolve the contradiction between waging a war against all Europe and establishing a stable government for France. "The Directory, with its two Councils, was only organized anarchy, and the conquest of natural frontiers was nothing but warfare erected into a system. Warfare and anarchy led a nation which sought order and victory into a military dictatorship."[51] That some general should seize power was inevitable. It chanced to be Bonaparte.

The Revolution, as a whole, perpetuated quite as much of the old order as it replaced. The very vices of the Revolution were a legacy of the monarchy it supplanted—the *raison d'état,* the war for natural frontiers, the tendency to absolute authority. Even the miserable mobs, by whose support the terrorists were able to seize control of the Revolution, had been a feature of the old society and had periodically erupted ever since the time of the Hundred Years' War. Finally, it was the sense of national unity and the realization that political liberty is the only guaranty of other liberties which eventually brought the Revolution to stability; and both of these principles had been elaborated under the *ancien régime*. The reaction of Europe to the Revolution was just as much in terms of an inherited pattern.[52]

Sorel departed in several respects from the conventions of the Opportunist analysis. The extent of his concern for the place of the Revolution, considered as an event in European history, set him apart from the other historians. He showed no sympathy for the Terror and made no effort to gloss over its pernicious effect on the

Revolution. He was much less preoccupied with justifying the Revolutionary war by reference to the counterrevolutionary interventionism, and much more concerned with the evil the war brought upon France.

But on the points which set the republicans into clearest opposition to the conservatives, Sorel took his stand with the left. The revolutionaries did not overthrow the old order chiefly because they had elaborated a philosophical system which was incompatible with monarchical society. They responded to a need for reform arising from the historic development of old France. The Revolution, as a whole, was more remarkable for its lasting and solid achievements than for the missteps it took in pursuing its forward course. Although enemies of social order gained an opportunity to work harm during the course of the Revolution, it does not follow that the Revolutionary principles must necessarily lead to socialism or a disruption of the foundations of society. They can be confined to their true content, civil and political liberty.

The manner in which Sorel's history retained a distinct and conservative character while forming part of the republican school suggests a parallel to the sort of development within the Third Republic which Thiers had led.

The division in French life between republicans and the counterrevolutionaries was sharp, yet there was a sort of middle ground. There was no effective alternate program between republicanism and royalism, but there was an important body of opinion which did not commit itself to either camp. Many Frenchmen of conservative convictions inclined towards the Republic but hesitated in their support for republicanism because it had for so long been associated with social upheaval and political instability. As time and events demonstrated that the Republic had been purged of its turbulence and popular radicalism, Thiers had begun to bring it the support of a large section of those' conservatives who had been distrustful of it, and the movement gained strength as time went on.

This development illuminates the position which Sorel held in relation to other republican historians and the kind of support which his interpretation gave to the Revolution and the Republic. Sorel endorsed the essentials of the Revolution, but he did not even profess admiration for the revolutionary populace and unequivocally condemned the Terror. The conservatives who were won over to the Third Republic did not seek to become leaders of the masses nor to glorify the common people: they were more than a little distrustful of those republicans who did. Sorel was not fascinated by the drama of the Revolution at grips with the combined forces of Europe's past nor did he extol the Revolutionary war as a work of human liberation. It was not the conservative republicans who led the protest at the military impotence of the Third Republic and the demand for a revival of the republican strength of the French nation.

But, for all the reservations which he entered against the Revolutionary and republican tradition, Sorel finally judged that the Revolution had been a work of progress and had established a regime of civil and political liberty on which an orderly society might flourish. The conservatives of Sorel's day did not assume as axiomatic that concessions to the principles of the Revolution would not lead to social disorder. But they did come to accept this as a proven hypothesis. When this had become clear, they took their place with the republicans against the counterrevolution.

CHAPTER FOUR

UNDER THE IMPERIAL REPUBLIC

THE STRUGGLE for and against the Republic, which had over-
shadowed French life from 1871 until into the 1890s, rose to a
peak in the Dreyfus affair, then receded from the foreground of
public attention.

By the time the Dreyfus affair had subsided, France had quitted the
nineteenth century. A group of forces which had been gaining strength
throughout the nineteenth century came to maturity in the 1890s and
basically modified the character of French national life.[1] The developments of these years brought a close to the first phase of the Third
Republic and, in more than a literal sense, to the nineteenth century
as well. The problems confronting France in the two decades before
the first World War were those of a twentieth-century empire.

The conflict over the form of government ceased to be an immediate
issue after the Dreyfus affair, although it was far from ended. The
antagonisms which had featured public life in the 1870s and 1880s were
summed up in *l'Affaire,* and party feeling on either side was never
more bitter in any of the earlier struggles. But even though the crisis
was so severe as to draw international attention, it was not accompanied by any serious revolutionary action. When the republican defense was finally entrenched in the Waldeck-Rousseau ministry, the
opposition to the Republic did not disappear. But the Republic was
thereafter free to move into the first World War and emerge through
it into the world of Versailles without again being directly challenged
by the France of the counterrevolution.

The position of France in its relations with other powers greatly
altered during this period. A sense of humiliation had borne on all

quarters of the French nation after the defeat of 1870–1871 had revealed its military impotence and diplomatic isolation. The army was reorganized and re-equipped in the succeeding decades and regained some of its lost respect. The system of alliances which began with the Franco-Russian agreement and eventually concluded in the *Entente cordiale* reinforced the diplomatic position of France. An evident sign of the resumption of French power on a world scale was the extensive colonial empire, which Ferry had given new vigor to expand in the 1880s and which continued to spread up to the eve of the World War.

French economic life developed in these years to a degree not matched in any equal span of its history.[2] Although the changes characteristic of the industrial revolution had been progressing throughout the century, the deep transformation of economic life they entailed was made most evident after the rapid acceleration which began in the 1890s. A heavy drag on the economy was removed with the passing of the Long Depression of 1873–1896, and business activity expanded rapidly. The extent of commercial exchanges, both within France and with other countries, and the quantity of goods involved increased at an unusually rapid rate. The processes of production were transformed concurrently by technical advances, especially as power was applied to machinery. The growth of the iron-working industries was both a part and a symptom of this trend. These developments necessarily brought with them increased concentration of control in bigger units. They further required that larger amounts of capital must be mobilized for such enterprises. The financiers who made this possible came to hold increasing power over those branches of capital which were concerned with manufacture or trade. The power of credit capital was closely associated as well with the export of capital goods to the colonial and world markets. The Bourse and the banks began to hold the key positions in the French economy.

This evolution left a mark on the social character of wealth. Property in land dropped to a place of relatively less influence in the measure that industry and finance gained power. The spreading range of "blind" capital, on the other hand, made it easier for families whose wealth was formerly invested in their estates to interest themselves in the business operations of the cities inasmuch as these no longer obliged the investor to participate in the management of affairs. So the wealth of the countryside tended to fuse with the urban, and the political and social power of the landed aristocracy lost its independent force.

As these developments made themselves felt and as the question of the republican form of government receded from the range of immediate issues, the politics of Parliament underwent a change. The core of the ministry was now chosen, as a matter of course, from the ranks of the republicans. The older republican factions did not substantially alter their program when they became the base of the government. They continued to stand for the defense of the democratic republic, the struggle against clerical influence, the championship of a kind of nationalism which was drawn from the Revolution but which was now imperialist as well, and they showed no marked concern for reform of the social order.

But the republicans had to pay a price for their possession of power by assuming responsibility for the course of governmental policy. The defense of republicanism against the counterrevolution, which had been their chief stock for the first twenty years or so of the Third Republic, became a poor substitute for a forward program after the Republic had been firmly established. When a considerable amount of corruption in Parliament came into the open after the republicans were established in power, it began to appear to some elements in the nation that the Republic was serving chiefly to endow the republicans in office. The scandal growing out of the finances of the French Panama Canal company was the most spectacular, but by no means the only revelation of its kind. Such corruption seemed to some sections of opinion to be a continuing process rather than a matter of only occasional criminal acts. The shock was so much the greater for France in that the men who had fought so long for the Republic had not only considered it a superior form of government, but had associated it with personal probity as well.

A reaction from parliamentary government gained strength as a consequence in the same years that saw the Republic most securely established. The movement did not present a critical danger to the

Republic until after the World War, but its underlying features were revealed during the pre-War generation. The gaining authoritarian tendencies on the right were a clear mark of this current. The growing socialist left, even though it supported the Republic against the right, expressed a repudiation of the older republicanism. The wide extension of syndicalism was an unequivocal attack from the left directed against the parliamentary system.

The triumph of the Republic and the beginnings of the reaction from republicanism were closely related to the rapid growth of the industrial working class, produced by the accelerated economic expansion, and to its organization in support of socialism. A socialist movement, alongside of the republican, can be traced back in French history as far as Babeuf or perhaps even to the Terror. During most of the nineteenth century it had secured small support from scattered elements in the nation; and its theory had been expressed in a number of diverse systems, none of which had gained general acceptance, even among socialists.

Marxism, which was ultimately to vanquish the other schools of socialism and to win the support of most of the working class of France, was slow in gaining ground. From 1850 until into the 1880s, the Marxists were competing, not only against the bourgeois republicans, but against other socialist groups and against the anarchists, led first by Proudhon and then by Bakunin. Among the leaders of the Paris Commune, there was only a small minority of socialists and scarcely more than a handful of Marxists. When socialist activity gradually resumed after the repression of the Commune, Marxism greatly improved its position.[3] A small band of workers, led by Jules Guesde, carried on a tireless work of agitation and propaganda in the cities during the late 1870s and the 1880s, and they finally established the dominance of Marxism among socialists. But the extension of socialism through the working class, still bound to the bourgeois republicans, was long impeded by bitter factional fights which for a time split the Marxists into five parties. These schisms abated sufficiently by 1896 to permit the socialists to mobilize a real mass following and send some fifty deputies to the Chamber in the elections of that year. The socialist parties from then on spoke as the representatives of the greater part of the working class and kept pace with its growth in succeeding years.

The question of the relations between socialists and bourgeois republicans gave great concern to the socialists, and no little travail to the republicans. Of the political issues which so divided the socialists, this was one of the most prominent. Socialists generally agreed that socialism demands a republican form of government. The reformists held, further, that socialists are required to co-operate with nonsocialist republicans in defense of the bourgeois republic. But the militants denied that there is any value for the working class in a republic which is acceptable to the bourgeoisie. Socialist forces had been split over this question when the political career of General Boulanger made the defense of the Republic an immediate issue. The Dreyfus affair, however, brought an organizational unity of socialists in defense of the Republic. But this agreement was almost immediately shattered when Millerand and his supporters attempted to extend it to an endorsement of participation by socialists in nonsocialist ministries. The reformists eventually had their way. All factions were gathered into one party in 1905, and the United Socialist Party persisted without rupture into the first World War.

The socialists hesitated less in giving support to the anticlericalism of the republicans. The reformists were not far removed from their republican allies in general outlook. The militants, who regularly assailed the reformists for co-operating with the republicans on other issues, did not especially object to such collaboration in curbing the power of the Church; they did not care even to present their case in terms of removing the political influence of the Church; they proclaimed their opposition to all religion.

On other issues, the relations of socialists and republicans were more complicated. The socialists were generally critical of imperialism, militarism, and nationalism. On specific issues involving these tendencies they often stood, either alone or in alliance with the left republicans, in opposition to government policy. But the socialists also showed a strong influence of nationalism and frequently their resistance in principle weakened in the test of action. The situation was further confused by the vacillations of the left republicans: they would shift against the socialists when the latter made conspicuous gains or when labor disputes turned into political issues. On the whole, the socialists tended to form an extreme left wing to the republicans rather than a revolutionary opposition.

The rapid spread of revolutionary syndicalism counterbalanced the movement of the socialists towards class collaboration in these years.⁴ Although the socialists, especially the Guesdist faction, had been largely instrumental in establishing the trade union movement in the 1880s, the syndicalists were able in the next decade to win large influence over the labor movement with comparative ease. Syndicalist theory may have given an impetus to the extension of unionism, even though its objective of a social revolution through a general strike never materialized. But the spread of syndicalism revealed that a considerable part of the working class had lost faith in the parliamentary Republic as a means of attaining social reform.

The republicans, even though they were firmly established in power, were thus under a real pressure from the left. The socialists supported the republicans against the right, but still they raised social and economic demands in behalf of a strong working class. The syndicalists, although they foreswore parliamentary politics, marked a radical temper within the trade unions.

Republicanism made some measure of adjustment to this pressure. The older republican factions did not attempt to modify their program. But the radical-socialist group emerged into prominence between them and the socialists. This new republican left was not sharply differentiated from the Gambetta left during the 1870s. But while the republicans of Gambetta's tendency had become centrists by the 1890s, the radical-socialists forwarded a demand for state intervention in the interests of the common people. They supported the second group of labor laws to be passed during the Third Republic, under the coalition ministry which liquidated the Dreyfus affair. They made a live issue of the proposal for an income tax, which Gambetta had raised even under the Second Empire but which had held little practical interest for his party. The radical-socialists were never in danger of losing themselves among the socialists on their left, however; they collided as often as they collaborated.

The older republican groups did not all look with equanimity on this leftward development. They had never admitted such social consequences to republicanism. The course of events seemed to bear out the charge which the right had been making for so long, that the Republic destroys the barriers to social upheaval. Republican deputies were now occupying benches well into the center. From this vantage point, many of them were able to discover the extent of their agreement with the deputies of the right, and the progression went even farther in a conservative direction.

The accession of republicans to the forces of the right was made the easier by a transformation which the right itself was undergoing.

The cause of the monarchy was now losing much of its effectiveness as a rallying point for the right.[5] The royalists, Orleanist and Legitimist, who had for so long made up the core of the right, had assented to most of the political demands of liberalism, but they held to the monarchy because they judged that it furnished resistance to the social disorder associated with republican liberalism. But the failure of the efforts towards restoration during the early years of the Republic seemed to demonstrate that the royalist cause was lost. By 1890, the old royalists were reduced not merely to a symbolic allegiance but to a wistful aspiration. When, further, the Vatican urged its followers to abandon systematic opposition to the Republic and to direct their efforts towards specific policies, the distinction between royalist and republican conservatives was further attenuated. The forces of the right increasingly bridged over the division on the juridical question of the form of government in order to secure the immediate interests of social conservatism.

An authoritarian tendency gained ground within the right, while liberal royalism was losing its strength. The older right, speaking characteristically in behalf of the values of a stable and rural life, had conceded most of the specific demands of the left, but held to the traditions of monarchy as a defense for the kind of social order familiar to its supporters. The newer elements of the right spoke from the experience of a turbulent urban national life. They demanded a government of authority which would forcefully maintain a conservative order in the face of the agitations of the left, and they repudiated the concessions which the older royalists had made to parliamentarism. While the earlier right had been so moderate in its nationalism that it had been reproached for sacrificing France to German hegemony and Catholic cosmopolitanism, the authoritarians strenuously exalted the French nation.

This new development was strikingly manifested during the Boulangist episode. The Boulangists demanded a strong government under an individual leader, supported by the popular will expressed through plebiscite, as against the ineffective and corrupt parliamentary regime; and they protested against French weakness before Germany and the world. The anti-Semitic campaign of Edouard Drumont and the organization by Paul Déroulède of the *Ligue des patriotes* during these years also revealed elements of the new right.

The *Action française* was one of the most notable expressions of modern royalism. The group of young royalists associated with the journal of that name, among whom Charles Maurras, Léon Daudet, and Jacques Bainville were outstanding, broke sharply with the earlier monarchists and attempted to rest their case simply on the need for authority in society as demonstrated by scientific sociological investigation and the demands of French glory; their monarchy might be restored by a sudden *coup* and need make no concession to parliamentary liberalism. The *Action française* group attracted wide attention, but it did not fully supplant the older royalists. Nor did it organize all of its own sympathizers, for many conservatives who were not royalists approved the viewpoint which the *Action française* group defended, but did not find it a ready instrument for practical political action.

The movement of conservative opinion towards authoritarianism and integral nationalism was an adjustment by the right to growing popular power in political life. The older royalists had conceded political liberalism but had relied on the monarchy and its traditions to restrain the operation of representative government. The modernists, aided in some measure by disillusionment with Parliament, brushed aside liberalism in the belief that the bonds of common national feeling would restrain social conflict. That the newer groups were drawing on a real source of strength was indicated by the measure of success General Boulanger was able to win.

The full force of this development, however, as well as that of the socialist left, was not to come until after the first World War.

The study of the Revolution reached its greatest intensity during this quarter-century preceding the first World War. The huge mass of documentary sources on the history of the Revolution, of which only scattered portions had been readily available to the early historians, was edited, and most of the important material was published during these years. The government of the Second Empire had created the *Archives parlementaires,* which was to republish material on the debates in the legislative assemblies of France since the Revolution. The series dealing with the period from the Consulate onward was begun in 1862. The series dealing with the earlier years of the Revolution began to appear in 1879. An important addition was made to the *Collection de documents inédits sur l'histoire de France* with the publication of the *Recueil des actes du Comité de salut public,* which Alphonse Aulard began to edit in 1889. The municipal council of Paris sponsored the publication of much material on the Revolutionary history of the city. Among the works in its collection were the *Actes de la Commune de Paris pendant la Révolution,* issued by Sigismond Lacroix between 1894 and 1914, and materials on the Jacobin society, edited by Aulard about the same time.

The economic history of the Revolution received serious attention during these years when contemporary public life was so largely occupied with problems arising from economic expansion. The extent of this interest was shown in 1903, when Parliament, at the instance of the socialist leader Jean Jaurès, authorized the publication of the *Collection de documents inédits sur l'histoire économique de la*

Révolution française. Important studies in this field were carried on during these years by Jaurès himself, and a large number of scholars, including Loutchisky, Marion, Gomel, Levasseur, Hayem, and others.

The industrious research into the sources which were thus being made available in increasing quantity gave rise to the establishment of societies and journals devoted to the history of the Revolution. *La Révolution française* began to appear in 1881. When the *Société de l'histoire de la Révolution française* was founded in 1888, it assumed responsibility for the publication and Aulard took over its editorship. The journal became an outstanding vehicle for monographic research and discussion of Revolutionary historiography. A short-lived *Revue de la Révolution* ran from 1883 to 1889. The emergence of a new tendency in Revolutionary historiography, identified with Albert Mathiez, led to the establishment of the *Société des études robespierristes* in 1908 and of the *Annales révolutionnaires.* The latter merged after the War with the *Revue historique de la Révolution,* which had been issued since 1910, and took the name *Annales historiques de la Révolution française.*

Four men among the many engaged in detailed research on Revolutionary history during these years received special public prominence for the general interpretations of the Revolution as a whole they published. Two of them, Alphonse Aulard and Louis Madelin, presented up-to-date versions of the basic analyses offered earlier by Taine and the Opportunist historians. Aulard's history gained general recognition as the authoritative expression of the viewpoint endorsed by the republicans then in charge of the government. Madelin restated the position of the conservatives in a form which could compete on more equal terms with Aulard's study than could the aging volumes of Taine.

The other two historians were innovators. Neither of them broke with his predecessors, but each contributed an analysis which was, to some extent, both original and characteristic of his times. Jean Jaurès, one of the leading spokesmen for the socialist movement now come to mature strength, presented a defense of the Revolution which was acceptable only in part to the republicans but which became an integral part of the theory of the socialist movement. Augustin Cochin stood in somewhat the same relation to the viewpoint of the right. Examining the Revolution in the light of contemporary experience with the workings of parliamentary politics, he found its condemnation not only in the spirit of social disintegration which it embodied, as Taine had suggested, but in the laws governing the operation of the parliamentary regime it created.

The first of these four writers to establish himself as a scholar in the field of Revolutionary history was Aulard (1849–1928). Aulard made the study of the Revolution his whole life-work.[6] He had attracted sufficient attention by 1895, when the municipal council of Paris endowed a professorship at the University, to gain appointment to the position. He remained there until his retirement. He was largely occupied in the publication of documents on the Revolution and was responsible for much monographic research on detailed aspects of its history. By 1901, when his general study of the political history of the Revolution was published,[7] he was widely acknowledged as the foremost authority on the subject then living.

The starting point of the Revolution appeared to Aulard, as it had to his predecessors, to lie in the need for reform implicit in the state of France in 1789. France was determined to rid itself of the abuses of the *ancien régime*. The old order could not reform itself[8] and would not sanction reform from below. But France did not yet realize this: revolutionary doctrines were so little developed in 1789 that not one political figure expressed a desire for a republic.[9]

The whole of the Revolution consists of the process by which France learned from experience that the reform begun in 1789 could not be completed until a democratic republic had been established.

The revolutionary middle class had some understanding of this when its representatives drew up the Declaration of Rights. They tried, however, to conceal the consequences of the Declaration behind a mask, to use their own figure. But "when the faults of the King rent the *mask,* when the pact between the nation and the King was definitely broken, experience led the French to follow out the implications of the Declaration by establishing the regime of 1792 and 1793, that is, democracy and the Republic."

— Even the peak of the Revolution formed part of the same empiric process. The Convention can not be set apart from the earlier phases of the Revolution and condemned by itself. "The men of 1792 and 1793 have been called renegades from the principles of 1789. It is true that, for the moment, they did violate freedom of the press, individual liberty, the guaranties of legal and normal justice. They did so because the Revolution was at war against Europe; they did so to destroy the old order and to benefit the new; they did so in order to save the essential principles of the Declaration." If there were any renegades among the revolutionaries, they would not be men of the Convention, who extended the Revolution to its full limits, but the men of 1789, who shrank back from the implications of their own principles. It is fairer, however, to recognize that "there were no renegades, only good Frenchmen who did their best under different circumstances at different moments in our political evolution."[10]

Among the events which led the nation forward from the constitutional monarchy to the Republic, the King's flight to Varennes and the Champs de Mars massacre were outstanding.[11] The first created a republican party in France; the second revealed the democratic. The decisive turn in events was the declaration of war by the Revolution on the old order in Europe. It was the war which carried the republican party to power, and the victories of the armies which gave it support.[12]

The Terror itself was produced by the war. The Revolution had governed with respect for law and liberty up to August, 1792. "Then, after the forces of the past had joined together and provoked a civil war and a foreign war in which the nation felt itself attacked, front and rear, and in mortal danger, then the Revolution covered its countenance, suspended the principles of '89, and turned against its enemies the violent measures of the old regime which they formerly employed against it. The suspension of the principles of '89 is what made the Terror, and that suspension became complete when the danger was greatest, and especially when Paris was most aware of that danger, when it suffered most from it, in August and September, 1793."[13]

The religious policy of the Convention, too, was rooted in the conditions of the war. The Revolution was not disposed against the Church from the outset, but was gradually turned against it by the connection between the Church and the counterrevolution. This was the source of the persecution of the priests who refused to subscribe to the Civil Constitution, and the origin of the cults of reason and the supreme being as well.[14]

The policy of expedients brought the Revolution to something of a working socialism.[15] This was certainly not due to socialist preconceptions: none of the revolutionists had any such purpose. It was the political exigencies of the war which brought forth progressive taxation, forced loans, laws to increase the ownership of land, and the laws of the maximum. The Terror contained something more than adaptation to war needs however. "It was doubtless a provisional structure for temporary circumstances. But when they built it, whether or not they knew it, the workmen incorporated plans and elements for the future and enduring city of normal times, which was to be a democratic city."[16]

Among the men who led the Revolution at its height, Danton was the true statesman. Marat had a real influence but was so extreme and intransigent as scarcely to be human.[17] Robespierre was merely a trimmer who offered no forward policy but managed to utilize currents of opinion for his own advancement.[18] Danton's consistent aim was conciliation. He did not identify himself with a definite program but, taking the situation as he found it, tried to operate within it for the interest of France and the Revolution. This dictated an end to the war at the earliest opportunity. It required at home the formation of a third party between Mountain and Gironde. To the achievement of these conditions, Danton sacrificed everything—truth, honor, and his own reputation.[19]

The continued pressure of the war destroyed Danton, for his purposes required peace, and swept Robespierre, the champion of the Revolutionary war, into power. But the same circumstances which had elevated Robespierre were after a time to dictate his fall. France rid itself of his tyranny just as soon as it was saved from the enemy without.[20]

The revolutionary government did not outlive Robespierre. The bourgeoisie took advantage of the Thermidorean crisis to destroy not only Robespierre but the popular forces, and to put itself in the place of the whole people. The continuation of the war had by this time corrupted the patriotism which originally gave it its character of a war of independence and freedom. By serving bourgeois interests and this corrupt patriotism, Bonaparte was able to make himself dictator.[21]

Aulard's study of the Revolution was a continuation of the work of the Opportunist historians. Aulard himself made this clear by indicating that Danton, whom he presented as the statesman of the Revolution, was the political ancestor of Gambetta.[22] Aulard gave a clearer and better organized form to the work of the earlier republican historians, and he rested it on a fuller study of the sources, but he did not depart from the outline they had used.

For Aulard, as for his predecessors, the Revolution was essentially the reaction of reasonable men to the circumstances in which they found themselves rather than the realization of reforms deduced theoretically from abstract premises.

Yet the Revolution transcends the immediate environment in which it was created and, indeed, is timeless and universal. Aulard makes this clear by distinguishing two usages of the phrase *French Revolution*. One is favored by those who are hostile to the Revolution: it includes under that term all that happened in the years of the Revolution. Such a definition makes the Revolution bear the guilt for everything reprehensible within the period, even for the crimes provoked by its enemies. The term *French Revolution,* properly speaking, denotes only the principles of the Revolution and acts which conform to them.[23] Those principles remain valid. They imply democracy and a republican government. They must prevail over the political pretensions of the Church.

To this extent, Aulard repeated the analysis of the Opportunist historians, just as contemporary republicans maintained a continuity with their predecessors of the early Republic.

But the meaning of the Revolution included social democracy as well as political: with this judgment Aulard passed beyond the position of the Opportunists. The course of the Revolution required the establishment of many measures of a socialist tendency, even though the revolutionaries were not predisposed in that direction. Even the principles of the Revolution give support to socialism as an organized body of doctrine. "These consequences, which would later be called *socialism,* were masked much longer than the political, and even today, only a small minority of Frenchmen has removed the mask. The majority, on the contrary, seeks, with sentiments of religious respect and terror, to fix it more firmly and to make it more concealing."[24]

The meaning of *equality,* as the word appears in the Declaration, gives the key to the social content of the Revolution. The authors did not hold that all men have the same strength of body and mind, nor that the state should attempt to create such an unnatural uniformity. But the Revolutionary affirmation of equality meant that the state should be so directed that further inequalities should not be added by the operation of laws and government to those which are natural. "One man is born more vigorous, more intelligent than another. Is it fair for him to find in his cradle, beyond that, a sum of money or a property in land which will double or triple his strength in the struggle for life? ... Is it just that, by the work of laws, there should be men who are rich at birth and others poor at birth?"[25] The principles of 1789, far from being opposed to socialism, contain a social program which is not yet achieved and which only later generations would realize.

But it was not the socialism of Marx's adherents that Aulard found in the Revolution. The social democracy of which he spoke meant an initial equality for all men, to be attained chiefly through taxation, in what would remain a competitive society. It was not presented as a forcible displacement of capitalist property by the working class, nor the social control and direction of productive forces. Aulard's Revolutionary socialism was equalitarian, not communist.

Aulard's acknowledgement of the social implications of the Revolution and his definition of them suggest the modification which contemporary republicans had made in the social viewpoint of the Opportunists. The republicans who were now in command of the government were the heirs of Gambetta. They were quite as bourgeois as the earlier left had been and just as much attached to capitalist economics.

But the demands of labor could not be ignored or denied then as they had in earlier years. A large part of the working class was now organized behind socialist parties for independent political action. The support of the socialists was often indispensible to the republicans. The pressure of the socialists and of the trade unions had forced the republicans to concede items of social legislation and to make the income tax a live issue in current politics. The republicans had thus been obliged to extend the program presented by the Opportunists, even though they considered themselves only their followers. But Gambetta had never been so much concerned with the demands of an organized labor and socialist movement nor had his fraternal rivals, Simon, Ferry, Freycinet, and the others.

So it was natural that the historian who carried on the tradition of the Opportunists in the interpretation of the Revolution should find in that crisis of French life the source of democratic republicanism and of the social republic which would achieve true equality by the intervention of the state as well. But it was to be expected, too, that, in his judgment, this social democracy would not conflict with capitalist modes of production.

The publication of Aulard's history of the Revolution in 1901 endowed the left with an up-to-date account by a scholar whose full acquaintance with the source material in his field could not be questioned. The right was therefore put at something of a disadvantage. Taine's history was by then more than twenty years old. It had been the product, moreover, of a rather brief research by a man who was not a professional historian of the Revolution. In view of the development of historical writing on the Revolution into an exacting profession, Taine's work now suffered in comparison to that of Aulard.

The deficiency was filled in 1911 by Louis Madelin, a man of conservative views who had made a career of historical research and who
was quite familiar with the recent contributions to the historiography
of the Revolution. His interpretation closely followed the pattern of
Taine's but was marked by a more moderate tone. He adhered more
strictly to the narrative of events and presented his judgments chiefly
in a lengthy epilogue, which clarified and summarized the argument
implicit in the preceding account.

The *ancien régime* itself had prepared the way for its destruction. —
The old order was outgrown by 1789. The king had lost his original
functions of liberator, defender, and magistrate. The services which
once justified the privileges of the higher estates were dead letters. The
ancien régime had become a spendthrift anarchy and was crushing the
peasantry. So "the Revolution of 1789 was the work of the nation. The
'advance of enlightenment' had opened the eyes of the upper classes to
the abuses of inequality. Excessive public misery had forced the popular classes to revolt. The firm will to abolish the feudal regime had
aroused the peasant. The evident anarchy holding sway over the royal
government had made everyone want a constitution: by that, nine-
tenths of the French meant only a charter which would at last organize
the state. Equality in respect to taxation and justice, abolition of the
feudal regime, methodically arranged administration—that is what
France wanted in 1789."[26]

The philosophy of the eighteenth century contributed to the Revolu- —
tion, even though it had real causes in the situation of the old order, by
undermining the power of the monarchy to resist. "Who, if not the
philosophers, did enfeeble authority, disarm the privileged classes, and,
even more, create a revolutionary state of mind within the young
bourgeoisie?"[27]

The legitimate purposes of the Revolution were accomplished by
August, 1789. The deputies of the National Assembly then embraced
one another and declared the Revolution closed.[28]

But it was impossible to bring the process to a halt so soon. It was
forced to a further point by those who wished to profit from it as individuals. A revolution "never proceeds without stirring up troubled

elements in the eddies. Every nation contains some such, at every epoch. There are ambitious politicians in lofty places; lower down, there are the moral and social outlaws; at every level, there are those who fish in muddy waters. On July 14, a young journalist had thrown a motley crowd of bandits against the Bastille of the *faubourg Saint-Antoine*. . . . The act seemed to win universal approval. From then on, rioting was consecrated: it was organized into a chronic state."[29] The adventurers who sought a personal profit from the Revolution broadened its scope in order to make room for their ambition.

The majority of Frenchmen did not approve of these agitators, but submitted to them in the belief "that they were the defenders of the conquests made in the summer of 1789, and that these conquests were threatened. Those who had been stirred up, those who had gained positions for themselves, the tribunes, the agitators in the Assembly and in the streets, found their best allies in the Court of Versailles and the former privileged classes."[30] These latter were of divided counsel, and by neither resisting firmly nor assuming leadership of the Revolution, they allowed the unsound elements to gain control of it. A great king at the head of the nation might have rescued his people from this fate, but Louis XVI, though personally virtuous, was quite incapable of dealing with a crisis of this magnitude.[31] Certainly he was unable to check the course of events after the army, his chief recourse and the *ultima ratio* of any government, was dissolved by the revolutionary spirit.

Such a state of affairs gave free rein to the revolutionaries. "The leaders of the integral revolution carried the Assembly, drunk with idealism, to formidable reforms. Everything was destroyed without consideration. A curious *Constitution,* a monument to utopia, was raised where nothing else was standing, while a splendid *Declaration* promised everything that was not contained in the Constitution and so condemned the Revolution never to be terminated. Perhaps the King might have put up with this. But the deputies, carried away by reforming madness, urged further onward by hatreds older than they, and finally beset by the need for money, turned towards the Church—

more ancient than the throne—and, at first with the idea of applying pressure to it, set to reforming it."[32]

It was this which forced the King into the arms of the emigration and entrenched the Revolution. The new proprietors of lands formerly belonging to the Church were now committed to defending the Revolution. At the same time, the emigration set itself the task of undoing the Revolution as well as halting it. When the aid of Europe was enlisted in this endeavor, the breach between France and its former authorities was further widened.[33] The extreme revolutionists were now able to call upon the support of French patriotism and to present themselves as men who would defend the fatherland and even extend it to its natural frontiers.

France, the Revolution, and the Republic all fell under the control of a small party. "Three-quarters of France were now hoping that the Revolution would be halted, or rather delivered from its odious exploiters. But the latter held the country in a thousand ways. Every time it tried to rise, it was subdued. . . . Since they could rule only through the use of the Terror, they struck whoever seemed at a given moment to wish to oppose the Terror, even the best servants of the Revolution. The men who had launched the idea of reforms in 1789 were thus decimated, then those who had founded the Republic in 1792, from Barnave to Danton."

Even in 1794, the nation still desired the legitimate reforms of the Revolution, that is, a government soundly organized according to the demands of the *Cahiers;* but it could not dislodge the oligarchy which had gained control of the state. "These Jacobins who had taken command no longer aimed at establishing any principles, but at defending forcible interests, their power, their fortunes, and, most important of all, their lives, for which they feared in the event of counterrevolution."[34]

The Terror did not take its victims exclusively from among the enemies of reform. Workmen, servants, and small shopkeepers suffered from it as well.[35] Beyond that, the economic distress induced by the Terror bore heavily on the workmen, who were denied all rights of redress, both by suffrage and by organized economic action.

The tyranny came to an end in the course of events: it could scarcely go on forever. Directly after Thermidor the Bourbons might quite possibly have been able to return to the throne, if they had not been so intransigent: they refused to guarantee the basic reforms of the Revolution.[36] So the makeshift of the Directory was devised. From 1795 on, a thousand conflicting wills converged in search of a personal government which would protect the accomplishments of the Revolution. Since the Bourbons spurned their opportunity, it fell to an ambitious general.

Madelin's interpretation thus followed the main scheme of Taine's. Both historians agreed that the old order was an outworn system of privileges which once had been balanced by duties but which by 1789 had become simply a burden on the nation. Reform was required at two points: control of taxation by representatives of the nation, and a rationalized administration. The Revolution had passed beyond these goals and was out of control by the end of the summer of 1789.

Madelin did not support Taine's emphasis on the role of the revolutionary doctrines, but did agree that the progress of the Revolution into the Terror was the work of a small band of self-seeking Jacobins who set up a tyranny over the nation by ruthless force. Madelin allowed a large weight to the circumstances in which the reformers found themselves and presented the men of the Revolution as opportunists and realists rather than doctrinaire theorists.[37] But the outcome of the Revolution was to enrich a small group of revolutionists at the expense of the nation. For all their harmony, however, the two accounts differed in tone. Taine presented the Revolution as the accomplishment of a determined minority in spite of the true nation, but his attack on the revolutionary populace which participated in the crises of the Revolution was of an unchecked intensity. The men who captured the Bastille, brought the royal family to Paris, and applauded the executions of the victims of the Terror were a rabble so deranged as to be scarcely human. The evil worked by the revolutionary spirit lay in that it dissolved the restraints which hold back this popular force. Madelin followed Taine in considering the revolutionary party a minority of the people and in condemning its actions, but he was not so greatly preoccupied with the ever-present threat of a scrofulous, epileptic, deranged mob. Nor did he find that the doctrines of reform were primarily responsible for the outbreak of the Revolution. Madelin more readily granted indulgence to the men of the Revolution, in view of their situation, and gave more attention to indicating the excesses of the Revolutionary period than to locating their evil source.

So it would be possible for a Frenchman to share Madelin's judgments on the Revolution, even though he might retain a certain warm regard for the Revolutionary tradition.

Just such a limited change had taken place since Taine's day in the conservative tendency in French social politics. The right, in both generations, accepted the basic reforms of the Revolution and did not aspire to restore the *ancien régime*. At the same time they both condemned social disorder or movements of equalitarian social reform urged in the name of the Revolution. The conservatives at the turn of the century, however, were confronted by the force of the popular classes, now so strongly organized in political life that they could no longer be ignored or attacked frontally. This force was formidable enough to bring many former republicans into alliance with the old royalist groups on the basis of general social conservatism.

The outlook of part of the right had, under the pressure of this development, become more conciliatory towards those who were thoroughly conservative but also respected the Revolutionary tradition. So it was not unusual in Madelin's time for conservatives to hold reservations in favor of the Revolution which would scarcely have been possible in Taine's day.

The emerging independent political strength of the working class was expressed primarily in the socialist movement. Since the middle of the 1890s, the socialist delegation in Parliament had been a considerable force, representing a mass following rather than a sect. The socialists had some difficulty in separating themselves from the republicans, inasmuch as they supported the existing Republic against attack from the right, joined in the struggle against clericalism, and even accepted capitalism as a framework within which to effect reforms.

But the socialists were successful in establishing their distinct identity at least on theoretical grounds, for the bourgeois republicans would hardly accept the doctrines of Marxism.

Socialist theory naturally gave large place to the history of the French Revolution, for it was one of the great social movements of modern times and, in Marxist terms, it established the preconditions for socialism itself. When Jean Jaurès, one of the chief spokesmen for the United Socialist Party, set to the task of editing an ambitious history of France which would give appropriate intellectual foundation for the new mass party, he reserved for himself the task of writing the volumes which would deal with the Great Revolution. Jaurès was quite prepared for such a work. He had long been interested in the history of the Revolution and had played a large part in directing attention towards the social and economic aspects of the material. His study was accordingly received with serious attention well beyond the ranks of the organized socialist movement.[38]

The position from which Jaurès considered the history of France was set forth at the outset. "It is from the socialist point of view that we mean to recount to the people, to the workers and peasants, the events which took place from 1789 to the end of the nineteenth century. We consider the French Revolution an immense work of admirable fecundity; but it is not, in our eyes, a definitive accomplishment, after which the only task remaining to history is endlessly to unfold its consequences. The French Revolution indirectly prepared the advent of the proletariat. It realized the two essential conditions for socialism: democracy and capitalism. But it was basically the political accession of the bourgeois class."[39]

The fundamental determinant for an individual is his economic occupation, and for a society, the economic structure underlying it; these general forces hold throughout the history of the French Revolution. But "in the course of the semimechanical evolution of economic and social forms, we will be pleased to give expression to that lofty dignity of the free spirit, liberated even from humanity by the eternal universe. The most intransigent Marxist theorists can not reproach us for this," for Marx himself recognized that economic forces operate only upon human beings.[40]

The revolutionary spirit was a powerful force in the Revolution, but its intellectual sources "would have been fruitless if there had not been a new social class interested in a great change and capable of producing it."[41] The development of capitalism had created that class, given it particular interests to defend, shaped its thinking, and endowed it with the strength to prevail over the older society: that was the true root of the Revolution. The forcible destruction of the old order could have been averted only if the King had set himself at the head of a reform movement directed against the privileged classes; and this condition was historically incapable of fulfillment.

The development of the Revolution during the period of the National Assembly was controlled by the middle class, but in spite of that —indeed, because of that—was progressive. The Declaration of Rights illustrates the situation. The affirmation of natural rights in this document expresses a great truth of lasting validity. The Declaration also shows limitations due to the position of the bourgeoisie whose representatives drew it up. But these are objectionable only outside their historic context. Consider bourgeois property, for example. This "appeared to the Constituents to be in harmony with natural liberty by virtue of its mobility and flexibility. There was no closed caste, no economic predestination: every man, whatever his origin, was free, within the bourgeois legal system, to own, build, trade. . . ."[42] The socialist criticism of bourgeois property rights would have been just as unanswerably correct then as it is now. But, by the nature of things, it could not be raised at that time: history had not yet made it a question of the day. It would be childish to hold it against the bourgeois revolutionaries that they were not twentieth-century socialists. In the circumstances of their times, they did in fact speak for all humanity.

The restricted suffrage of the early Revolution is to be understood in the same way. "What was the exact feeling which moved the revolutionary bourgeoisie on that question of suffrage right? I believe it is excessive and premature to credit it with a very clear class antagonism towards the proletarians. No more than the proletariat had yet a clearly marked force as a class did the bourgeoisie have a quickened distrust for it. . . . I will say that it was the sub-proletariat of the times, rather than the proletariat itself, that was set aside."[43] Fear of the effects of counterrevolutionary demagogy was what prompted the restriction.

Even the Le Chapelier law forbidding trade union action by workmen, the most extreme measure directed against the proletariat, did not arise from a class struggle between bourgeoisie and proletariat.[44] It aroused little discussion of any sort at the time and was not opposed by men like Marat and Robespierre, who regularly championed the rights of the common people. During the Terror, at the height of popular power, the Le Chapelier law was not deemed important enough to repeal.

The principal shortcoming of the National Assembly was that it did not sufficiently prosecute the attack on the old order: that task it left to the Legislative. "The uncertainty, the hesitation of the Legislative arose from this: the classes directing the Revolution were still monarchist, and the monarch was determined to betray the Revolution. The historic function of the Legislative was to put an end to that scandalous and mortal contradiction."[45]

The Legislative sought to solve its problem through a war against monarchical Europe. Scarcely any decision in the Revolution was more crucial, for the evil effects of that war had not played themselves out a full century later. They included the eventual *dénouement* of the Revolution in a bloody caesarism, a loss of liberty for France which was not fully regained until 1871, and the national animosities and militarism which were pressing on France at the beginning of the twentieth century.[46]

The resolution for war was a mixture of inevitability and choice. The Revolution presented a threat to the established order of all Europe which the foreign monarchs could not ignore: that they should entertain a common hostility to the Revolution could not be avoided.[47] But on the other hand, these sovereigns did not want open warfare and had so many divergent ambitions that they might well have been prevented from taking united and effective action against France.[48]

The proper policy for the revolutionists, by no means impossible of achievement, would have been to avoid giving occasion for such a unity of the old order. A vigilant pressure on the King would have forced him to accept ministers devoted to the cause of reform, while the propaganda of the ideas of democracy would have built up support for the Revolution abroad. If war had then been found inevitable, at least it would have been entered upon with more favorable auspices.[49]

The decision for war was actually taken in quite a different fashion. The ministers who were hostile to the Revolution were not forced from their positions of power. Precisely because the counterrevolutionary forces were so strong within France, Brissot and the war party urged the declaration. This demand reflected a lack of confidence in the strength of the popular forces, for the Brissotins argued that only in the heat of war could the internal enemies of the Revolution be destroyed.[50] But those few revolutionaries who opposed the declaration betrayed the same lack of faith in the Revolutionary cause, for they opposed the war on the grounds that it would necessarily be directed by traitors: they were not confident that the people could break the power of the Court party.

The war to which the Legislative looked for a solution of its difficulties proved to mean the end of the Legislative itself. The insurrection of August, 1792, which terminated its career, again reveals the relation between the working class and the bourgeois revolution. "The workers, the proletarians who fought alongside of the revolutionary bourgeoisie, did not formulate any economic demand. Even earlier, when they were fighting against the forestallers and monopolists who had raised the price of sugar and other commodities, the Parisian workers used to say: 'We are not women, teasing for candies; we are fighting so as not to leave the Revolution in the hands of a new caste which is selfish and oppressive.' . . . The proletarians well knew that the whole exaltation of national life and liberty would be an elevation of their strength, and they had a dark presentiment of the future of society. But their conscious thought went directly to the fatherland menaced by the foreigner, to liberty betrayed by the duplicity of the King."[51]

When the Girondins proved incapable of leading the national effort, the Convention passed into the hands of the Jacobins. The deficiency of the Girondins was not that they were too firmly attached to federalist theory nor that they were especially limited to the defense of bourgeois class interests.[52] Their party spirit had simply degenerated into factionalism and exclusive sectarianism; thereby they became a negative force. The Jacobins were not hostile to the bourgeoisie in principle nor even notably concerned with social problems. But they were intensely devoted to the success of the Revolution and were prepared to take all necessary measures, including social and economic, in order to win the war.

The Terror, which marked the height of the Revolution, revealed its failure as well.[53] The revolutionists were not able to find a common ground on which to co-ordinate their efforts, on which to found the Revolution in a lasting form. It was this failure, rather than the effusion of blood which was only its consequence, that is the real tragedy of the Revolution.

Even when Robespierre emerged as the unchallenged master of France, he failed to bring the Revolution to a kind of normality while defending it from its enemies. The needs of the situation required the government to indicate to Europe that France would make peace with any power that recognized the Republic, to establish that the *assignats* would be redeemed immediately after the war, and thereby to remove the cause of the price rise which had necessitated the economic Terror.[54] But Robespierre did not measure up to the situation: he could only extend the Terror by the law of Prairial in the hope that by so doing he could shorten it. "From then on, by any hypothesis, Robespierre was lost. That law showed that he no longer was adequate to the immensity of the problem and of events and that the very void left by the disappearance of his adversaries made him dizzy."[55]

In the historiography of the Revolution, as in contemporary politics, the socialists thus made a common front with the republicans against the right, yet remained separate from their allies.

For Jaurès, as for the republican historians, the Revolution was one block, to be defended as a continuous whole. Its origin lay in the material conditions of the times, and the revolutionary ideology drew its vitality from the material forces which supported it. The rationalism of the Revolution, its assertion of the natural rights of man, its democratic and nationalist elevation of the common people were all endorsed. Where the republicans were sometimes equivocal in their support of the Revolution against the claims of the Church, Jaurès avowed an antireligious atheism. "Those who, like us, want not only the complete laicity of the state, but the disappearance of the Church itself and of Christianity . . ." endorse the Revolutionary settlement of the relations of Church and state and regret only that it did not go further.[56]

The socialists in contemporary France similarly backed up the republicans in the conflict against the counterrevolutionary right: their support was considerable during the Boulangist campaign and even more substantial during the Dreyfus affair; and they lent important assistance in the conflict centering in the abrogation of the Concordat.

But the socialists presented their defense of republicanism as a stage towards a transformation of the bases of social life. The embodiment of the Revolution in the Third Republic was not the culmination of political and social progress; it was only the perfected instrument for a transition to a classless and socialist order. The socialists were divided among themselves on the method for accomplishing this further development, but they agreed that their objective lay beyond the bourgeois republic.

The socialists set analogous limits to the historical validity of the Revolution in a manner to which the republicans could not assent. In the socialist view, the Revolution was the work of a class which was justified in speaking for the whole people only by the historic fact that, at the stage of development prevailing at the end of the eighteenth century, it alone could organize the further advance of the nation. But that situation no longer obtained. History had passed beyond the point where the bourgeoisie led the whole nation. This role was now to be filled by the working class, and its task was to destroy the capitalism which the Revolutionary bourgeoisie had defended. The proletariat carried on the work of the bourgeoisie only in taking over from it the responsibility for progress.

Such a position inextricably mingled the analysis of the historical events with a program for modern France.

Jaurès's study further reflected socialist policy in its treatment of the Revolutionary war. Jaurès won international attention in the years preceding the first World War for his leadership of socialist forces in resisting militarism and in the struggle against the approaching war. It was natural, therefore, that he should devote extended consideration to the war in which Revolutionary France had been involved and that he should find cause for regret that it had not developed a policy which might have averted the war while it still waged its fight against the counterrevolution.

Quite as much as the republican and conservative interpretations, therefore, the socialist analysis of the Revolution ran parallel to the contemporary position of the party and formed an integral part of its ideology.

In much the same way that Jaurès had extended the former left analysis of the Revolution, Augustin Cochin presented an interpretation that followed in the direction of his rightist predecessors, but passed beyond the limits of their viewpoint.

Cochin (1876–1916) came of an aristocratic family long identified with the right. While he was still a young man, he established a reputation by his contributions to the conservative criticism of the Revolution. Cochin made a conspicuous entry into the controversial field of Revolutionary historiography by opening a frontal attack on Aulard. In 1908, Aulard published a criticism of Taine's history of the Revolution.[57] From an analysis of Taine's method of work, of the accuracy of his documentation and of the plausibility of his interpretation, Aulard sought to remove any claim which Taine might have to serious repute as an historian. The next year, Cochin published a rejoinder to Aulard in which he attempted to find as many inaccuracies in Aulard's critique as Aulard claimed to have found in Taine's history.[58] He concluded that Aulard had not successfully impugned Taine's scholarship, and proceeded further to offer a brief sketch of what he considered the proper approach to the problem of the Revolution. In the course of the next few years, he published further monographs and essays, but his death in the War ended his career before he had brought his work to a natural completion with a full-length history of the Revolution. Although much of his thought must therefore be inferred from the fragments which he made public, his writings exerted a real influence on conservative thought on the Revolution.

Opinion on the Revolution, Cochin pointed out, falls into two great divisions. He gave them names which have remained current: the conspiracy thesis (*thèse de complot*) and the circumstance thesis (*thèse de circonstances*). Both of these contain a measure of truth and neither adequately explains the Revolution.

The circumstance thesis was paraphrased by Cochin as follows: "The Revolution did not 'begin'; it never acted save under pressure of external circumstances which it could not even foresee: such is the thesis of all its defenders. This tends to prove that the ideas, the sentiments of the men of '93 contain nothing out of the ordinary in themselves; that if their acts shock us, it is because we forget their dangers, 'the circumstances'; and that any man of intelligence who was in their place would have acted as they did. It follows that sentiments which are so natural must necessarily have been widely held, and that terrorism was the work of all France, not of a minority."[59]

Such an explanation does not do justice to the revolutionaries, for their regime was quite as principled as the most legal *Parlement*. The core of their rationale was the defense of pure democracy, in which the people themselves exercise sovereignty.[60] Since the people can not actually attend to every detail of administration, a perpetual vigil must be kept over those who govern in behalf of the people through political clubs and associations. "Once it is granted that the people ought to reign by themselves, how can they do so unless they ceaselessly deliberate and vote? So permanent deliberating societies are founded in place of temporary electoral assemblies. These lead to a correspondence to exchange opinions and to the creation of a center to receive them: the central society. This is the Jacobin organization or, if you please, the Birmingham 'Caucus,' the American 'Machine,' our Grand Orient, . . . our C.G.T., or any other society of equals—philosophical, political, labor."[61]

This is the very heart of the Revolution. From such principles, and not from circumstances of any kind, "proceed all the frightening attributes of the new regime: the unlimited right over life and property, the accumulation of all powers in the same hands."[62]

The conspiracy thesis begins with a true perception of the nature of the Revolution. "This is the distinction as far back as one goes, then the divergence, then the conflict between the People, Sovereign of the Societies, and the people—between M. Aulard's Revolutionary France and simply France. The popular societies, the vital organ of pure democracy, are not the people—that is the truth which burst forth in Thermidor."[63] The Convention found itself, as the result of an occult influence, voting for and supporting measures which its members did not want nor approve.[64] Naturally, therefore, when the tide of the Revolution had passed, those figures who had been most conspicuous during the Terror were made to bear responsibility for it. The argument was from the fact of tyranny to the presumed existence of tyrants.

The thesis is incorrect, though, for the men who stood out in the period of the Terror were not tyrants. "There was undoubtedly oppression under the social regime, and oppression of the majority, but there was no fraud, no diversion of the power of the community to the profit of one man or one party. . . . The Jacobins rightly denounced factions: they were not a faction. They reigned neither for nor by themselves, but by virtue of an impersonal force which they served but did not understand and which would effortlessly destroy them, just as it had raised them up."[65]

Taine had approached an understanding that there was a force at work in the Revolution quite outside the area of individual responsibilities.[66] That was why he would apparently digress from the narrative to examine the crowd as a social phenomenon and why, lacking a better vocabulary, he had recourse to words like "disease" and "virus."

The key which Taine groped for and almost found is furnished by modern sociology in the scientific study of the conditions under which a society operates. Contemporary political life is replete with cases in which the same sociological process is at work. The most common examples are the political machines and pressure groups. Such societies are voluntary associations of men who share certain opinions, and their activity proceeds through agreement in terms of principles. The conditions under which such societies operate place a penalty upon a member in the degree to which he has interests, preoccupations, and commitments of his time outside the society, that is, in real life. Accordingly, advancement in such societies falls to those who have the least contact with reality.

Such societies were the real directing force in French life from the middle of the eighteenth century. Even "before the bloody Terror of 1793, there was a dry Terror in the republic of letters from 1765 to 1780, of which the Encyclopedia was the Committee of Public Safety and d'Alembert, the Robespierre. It mowed down reputations as the other did heads; its guillotine was defamation, 'infamy,' as the expression went."[67]

The effectiveness with which the *sociétés de pensée* controlled public life could not be proven more conclusively than by the uniformity of the *Cahiers* that were drawn up in 1789. From one corner of France to the other, in spite of all local differences, the *Cahiers* presented the same ideas in the same terms, even with the same copyist's errors.[68] Such uniformity could result only from the action of a network of societies.

Political liberty was steadily extended during the Revolution because it was a necessary condition for the rule of the societies. The more formal freedom the sovereign people enjoy, the less capable they are of making real use of it. The societies thereby gain a stronger control of affairs.[69] So the societies naturally forced France forward to the democratic republic.

The increasing power of the societies necessarily entailed a restriction of the area in which individuals are autonomous.[70] The social control of thought which had marked the pre-Revolutionary period soon passed into control of personal actions. Its final result was the socialization of property. This was effected through suppression of the grain trade, the laws of maximum and universal requisitions. "It was the end of the regime of individuals, for the common people as for the prince, in the fields, the workshops, and the counting-houses as in the Louvre."[71]

The nation as a unity fared no better than individuals, for the Revolution degraded even patriotism. For true French Patriotism, it substituted a Humanitarian Patriotism that was entirely subservient to the cause of the revolutionary societies. "That Patriotism centered in the *Parlements* in 1788 so as to enroll the towns, and in the Nation in 1789 in order to dissolve the provinces and corporations. It was not confined to those limits. As M. Aulard has well said, it was concerned for all Europe in 1791, just before the war; the Jacobins then saw themselves at the head of a European republic. If their Patriotism did come to a halt midway, fixed for a time to French unity, that was for fortuitous reasons: because the French provinces had yielded to Jacobin unity, and the foreign nations had resisted it. If it did defend the French frontiers, that was because they happened then to be the boundaries of the Humanitarian Revolution. But that was only by chance."[72] True French Patriotism had been put to unworthy uses before, by vainglorious monarchs, and it was to be misused again in later days.[73]

The end point of the Revolution was reached when men were entirely reduced to a wretched and defenseless isolation. "There is no example in history of a more profound and complete social dissolution. Free thought killed society because it killed the human person. Dissociating man and isolating him from every natural or moral attachment, it turned him loose, like a wreck on the tides of society. In his soul it left only that ruin, selfishness, which was called reason and which would turn into hatred or fear." The Revolution made France "a joint-stock company, a socialism of economic interests, and made of the nation, a trade union of egoisms."[74]

That Cochin's interpretation was derived from Taine's, he himself acknowledged. The roots of the Revolution were in the ideas associated with eighteenth-century philosophy, in abstract and reforming reason. There were real abuses to be corrected in the *ancien régime*, but these did not require an upheaval comparable to that which took place nor did they in fact generate it. The Revolution was not the work of the majority of the French, but was forced upon the nation against its will. It began as an attempt to accomplish a number of concrete reforms which all France recognized as necessary, but it quickly passed out of control. It eventuated in an unlimited attack on personal liberty, on property rights, on religious faith, on all the traditional institutions which mediate between the citizen and the state and within which man may live his life and sustain his individual personality.

This position, which Cochin shared with Taine, was common to the general outlook of the right in both generations. The right consistently opposed the use of the Revolutionary tradition to buttress the demands of the left when they were forwarded by a self-confident middle class. The hostility of the right to this use of the principles of the Revolution was not lessened when they became a justification for pragmatic social reform or the pretensions of proletarian socialism.

But Cochin diverged from Taine in point of focus. The lesson which Taine drew from the Revolution was that if its doctrines are allowed to pass as valid, they disarm the superior classes and loose the destructive force latent in the masses. Cochin's analysis was not so much concerned with the explosive potentiality of the common people as with the self-defeating nature of popular sovereignty. Cochin did not argue directly that the people should not themselves exercise state power, but that they could not. Political liberalism simply made the whole nation the victims of those who devoted their lives to the manipulation of political power. The political societies which actually control the state under a democracy are so constituted that they necessarily lead to the utmost extension of social control and the complete extinction of the rights of individuals.

Cochin's analysis of the Revolution is clearly related to an important current in the social thought of the conservatives of his day.

The right, which once had accepted most liberal political institutions, was then turning away from them. The change was not concerted nor universal, but it was appreciable. An ideological tendency was gaining which, instead of yielding to liberalism and opposing democracy, rejected parliamentarism but did not resist mass support.

Conservatives of this sort did not explicitly deny the right of the people to participate in political life, but they argued that parliamentary government was a deception by which politicians were endowed with the full state power while they pretended to act only in behalf of the people. They found that, instead of running counter to the growing popular forces of the day, they could thus draw a measure of support for the right from them.

This illusory character of parliamentary government was precisely the lesson that Cochin found in the experience of the Revolution. It was in the data of parliamentary democracy under the Third Republic, furthermore, that he avowed that his historical study was to be verified.

CHAPTER FIVE

AS THE REPUBLIC GREW OLDER

A s THE French Republic entered the first World War, it attained a greater degree of national unity than at any time in its earlier history.[1] For no effective group in French life did the war present primarily an issue of social politics: it was considered one of national interest. The right, which was in opposition when the war broke out, had by then become an energetic champion of French nationalism and could support the war more readily than any other policy which the government of the left might adopt. For the republicans, the war was the continuation of a diplomacy for which they themselves bore the responsibility. While they may not have wanted the war, they could not disavow it once it had broken out. The socialists might have been expected to oppose it, but socialist policy under the leadership of the reformists had generally been nationalist, and the appeal to defend France against the Germans would have been sufficient to win their endorsement, without the call to defend the Republic against an autocratic enemy.

This unity disintegrated as the war came to an end. The beginning of the dissolution may be discerned even in the course of the war. As the problems of post-War settlement came to the forefront, they were linked with contradictory systems of social politics whose conflicts long antedated the War. The polarizing tendency of French life resumed, and it dominated the career of the Third Republic for the twenty years that remained to it.

The Republic apparently held a more secure position shortly after the War than it ever had before. Republicans controlled the government; French economy had largely repaired the war damage and advanced, in important respects, beyond its pre-War level; French military power was unchallenged; and the French Republic seemed to control the destiny of a Europe made republican through its victorious efforts. The leftward current which brought socialist revolutions to much of central and eastern Europe did not directly threaten republican government in France; it did not take on a form comparable even to that of the British general strike. Nor did the opposition of the right, although it was fierce and unrelenting, break out in an immediate and clear-cut challenge to the Republic. The Third Republic was eventually destroyed, not by an open revolution, but by the fusion of its domestic struggles with their international manifestation in the course of the second World War.

The separation of forces on either side of republicanism nonetheless continued throughout the twenty years between World Wars. The first World War itself did not produce this division nor directly modify it, but the War and its aftereffects sharpened the conflict and intensified the crises in which the struggle was revealed. The early contest between royalists and republicans had been transformed in the generation before the War. It was then that the socialist movement was firmly established on the left of the republicans, that the right began to turn towards nationalist and antiliberal authoritarianism, and that republicanism became a centrist rather than a left wing political force. These developments were greatly quickened by the disillusionment consequent on the War, the grave economic crisis it precipitated, and the international political and social upheaval it aroused.

The forces of the left gained strength when the Communist Party of France made its entry, beyond the Socialist Party. The Communists made deep inroads on the older party at the Tours Congress of 1920 and continued to present a serious threat to the Socialists in later years. The Socialist Party successfully withstood the gains of its new rival and subsequently advanced to a position of first-rank power and influence. It became a governmental party and gave indispensable assistance to the republicans in several crises during the post-War period. But even though the Socialists no longer occupied the extreme left and gave such help to the republicans, they represented a strong force on the left of republicanism. Their pressure was especially powerful when they made a common front with the Communists.

The concurrent gains of the right were largely a consequence of this pressure from the left. The older representatives of the right, who had long argued that republicanism would lead to socialism, were strengthened in their convictions as their prophecy was apparently being verified. This turn of events held a cogency as well for many who would formerly have considered themselves champions of the Republic. So the current from the republican left to the socialist left was matched by a movement from republicanism to the right.

The close association of industrial and financial interests with the parties of the right was taken as a matter of course by this time. The right had included representatives of business interests since well before the Third Republic, but it had not been their characteristic political expression; the republican parties had more commonly served that function, while the royalists were typically associated with landed aristocracy. The economic expansion at the end of the nineteenth century altered that situation. The growth of large industry, closely bound to finance capital, destroyed the independent power of the aristocratic landowners. The men who owned or directed these new enterprises were acutely aware of the extent to which the working class was gaining united strength, and they naturally took responsibility for the interests of conservatism.

The right was not held together during the last years of the Third Republic by a unified body of ideas; it joined diverse groups through their common opposition to the left. The older royalism of the nineteenth century had almost disappeared. The King, the Church, a stable social hierarchy, and respect for tradition did not afford a program for post-War France. The newer royalism, of which the *Action française* was a chief proponent, attracted some interest and support in intellectual circles, but it did not gain sufficient following to give it first-rank political force. It was more remarkable as a clear expression of the integral nationalism and authoritarianism which were becoming the mark of the right. Openly fascist doctrines were adopted by a number of groups, including the *Jeunesse patriote* and the *Croix de feu*. None of these succeeded in drawing together the forces of the right, however; and while the extent of their power was not made clear, it certainly did not approach the level reached in other great nations of western Europe. Down to the end of the Republic, the right continued to represent a negative force, unable to agree on a forward program but united in resisting the progress of those parties of the left which proposed further to extend the work of the French Revolution.

The republicans now found themselves occupying an harassed center, beset by strong opposition on right and left. Their problem, throughout these twenty years, was to restrain the right, which would willingly destroy the Republic in order to defeat the left, and, at the same time, to check the left, whose social program was quite as objectionable to the republicans. In their efforts to maintain the middle course, the republicans continually shifted from alliance with the right to alliance with the left, but their career revealed an unresolved contradiction between the conservative criticism of republicanism and the socialist conception of it.

For post-War France, thus in a state of permanent crisis, the question of the meaning of the Revolution and the value of its legacy for the contemporary world assumed an indubitable urgency. The historical studies of the Revolution presented during this period did not belie the pertinence of the subject to the times. The judgments of historians followed closely the divisions on contemporary politics and supplied interpretations of the Revolution which formed integral parts of the conservative, republican, and socialist ideologies.

Current work on the Revolution was not, however, commonly directed towards the publication of full-length histories. Since the last years of the nineteenth century, when history had become a profession and tried to become an exact science, historical research had been increasingly absorbed in detailed examination of source materials and monographic discussion of particular problems. By the post-War years, this development had progressed so far that very few general histories of the Revolution appeared, even though research was proceeding with great energy and substantial results. The most notable advance was in the economic history of the Revolutionary period and the preceding years during which the Revolution was prepared. Outstanding contributions were made by Lefebvre, Labrousse, Braesch, Hauser, Sée, and a number of other scholars.

The four interpretive studies of the whole Revolution which achieved importance during the 1920s and 1930s split along the same lines as the works of the pre-War years. Albert Mathiez, a former pupil of Aulard who broke with the republican master and became his foremost rival, published a general history which followed in succession from that of Jaurès. The republican tradition was carried on in two co-operative histories. These latter were not published simply as studies of the Revolution, but as volumes in larger series; their authors, furthermore, had established their fame through monographic research, like Mathiez, and not through synthetic efforts. The conservative viewpoint was presented in a study by Pierre Gaxotte which combined the analysis of Taine and Cochin but did not purport to be a product of serious research.

Although Albert Mathiez (1874–1932) first made his reputation while a student under Aulard, he began to differ from his teacher during the early years of the century. Their disagreement was symbolized in contradictory estimates of Danton and Robespierre, but actually reflected the cleavage between republican and socialist viewpoints. The breach was widened when Mathiez became the center of a school of historical workers. Mathiez and his followers founded in 1908 the *Société des études robespierristes,* which in turn sponsored a journal and other publications in support of their viewpoint. The controversy led to personal bitterness, not only between Aulard and Mathiez, but also among their adherents.[2] Mathiez, professing a scientific detachment, did not make clear to what extent he considered that his interpretation was socialist. But the left took his work for a support to its position, and Mathiez gave strength to this reputation in the early 1920s, when he assumed responsibility for the publication of a new edition of Jaurès's history of the Revolution and acknowledged his indebtedness to Jaurès's studies.

The basic cause of the Revolution, as Mathiez presented it,[3] lay in material circumstances. "The French Revolution, whose irresistible suddenness surprised its authors and beneficiaries as much as its victims, was slowly prepared during more than a century. It arose from the divorce, which grew more profound each day, between reality and law, between institutions and customs, between the letter and the spirit. Those who were responsible for production, upon whom the life of society depended, daily increased their power, but labor continued to be treated, through social convention, as a shameful thing. Nobility was measured by uselessness. Leisure and high birth carried with them privileges which grew ever less bearable for those who created and accumulated wealth."[4]

The bourgeoisie that made the Revolution was far from being carried away by empty doctrines: it was acutely aware of realities and entirely competent to adjust its interests to them.[5] In the process of serving its own interests, the bourgeoisie was forced, by the circumstances of the times, to carry forward a work of progress. This situation was illustrated in the Declaration of Rights, the formal apology of the revolutionary bourgeoisie. In that document, it boldly "guaranteed 'resistance to oppression,' that is, it justified the revolt which had just triumphed, without being afraid that this might justify in advance other revolts still to come." Yet the Declaration revealed the limitations which its class character imposed on it. "It was a work of the bourgeoisie, and it bore the mark of the bourgeoisie. It proclaimed equality, but only a limited equality, subordinated to 'social utility.' It gave formal recognition only to equality before the law, equality in taxation, and the equal eligibility for positions of all who were qualified for them by their capabilities. It overlooked the fact that capabilities themselves depend on wealth and that, in turn, depends on birth, because of inheritance laws."[6]

The bourgeois character of the early Revolution did not mean that the middle class bore an animus against the common people. The exclusion of the masses from power simply reflected the belief that only the middle class was prepared to guide the Revolution, but the whole nation was expected to benefit from it. If the members of the Constituent Assembly "entrusted political, administrative, and judicial power to the bourgeoisie, it was not solely because of class interest, but because they thought that the people, still generally illiterate, would not have been capable of taking the helm. Popular education still lay in the future."[7]

The Revolution came into conflict with the Church, in the first instance, because of economic necessity. The primary problem of the Revolution was financial, and financial reform required a limitation of privileges of the Church.[8] There was no effort at the outset towards a separation of Church and state, for such a measure would have been impossibly in advance of general opinion. But as the Revolution progressed, the two powers came into sharper conflict and the Revolution then assumed a definite hostility to the Church. "Little by little, a sort of national religion was elaborated, a religion of the fatherland, which was still mingled with the official religion . . . , but which free spirits later attempted to detach and endow with an independent life."[9]

The declaration of war was one of the decisive actions of the Revolution. Mathiez generally shared the views of Jaurès on this issue.[10] Although circumstances made war likely, the Gironde did not take proper measures to avoid it, and therefore must bear a large responsibility for it. If the Gironde, from the first day, "had invoked the national interest to pardon the King, if it had boldly declared that his trial would prevent peace, . . . then it might have been able to bring the negotiations which had been opened to a favorable conclusion. Peace would have been possible on the basis of the *status quo*."[11] The leaders of the Mountain who stood out against the war lessened the virtue of their position by failing to present a concrete and precise alternative policy. Then they destroyed a necessary precondition for the maintenance of peace by demanding the trial of Louis XVI.

When the course of the war eventually brought the uprising of August-September, 1792, the first in which a popular insurrection challenged a representative assembly instead of supporting it, the conflict between the Gironde and the Mountain moved into the foreground. Their rivalry was more than simply political: it became a kind of class struggle with which the whole fate of the Revolution was bound up. "The opposition of programs expressed a basic opposition of interests and almost a class struggle. The Commune and the Mountain, which derived from it, represented the popular classes (artisans, workers, consumers) which were suffering from the war and its consequences: the high cost of living, unemployment, disequilibrium of wages. The Assembly and the Gironde, its heir, represented the commercial and well-established bourgeoisie, which was intent on defending its property against the limitations, the shackles, the confiscations with which it felt threatened."[12]

The class character of this struggle was qualified in that the Mountain did not represent a separate class, distinct from the bourgeoisie, but only a different orientation within the same class. "The majority of the partisans of the Mountain were, indeed, of bourgeois origin, like the Girondins. The class policy which they inaugurated did not issue wholly from the bowels of the people. It was a policy of circumstance, a plebeian way, as Karl Marx put it, of making an end of kings, priests, nobles, and all the enemies of the Revolution."[13]

The forward course of the Revolution necessarily brought about the defeat of the Gironde and the victory of the Mountain. "Between the Mountain, which identified itself with the Republic, and Royalism, allied to the enemy, there was no room for a third party. If the federalist revolt, the expression of the rancor of politicians who had fallen from power and of class selfishness, had been able to succeed, it would surely have led to the restoration of the monarchy."[14]

The fall of the Gironde gave a further impetus to the social policy of the Mountain. The Girondist revolt caused the people for the first time to look for enemies of the Revolution among those who professed to be its champions, as well as among the royalists; and since the Gironde had been supported by wealthy classes, its defection created the presumption that wealth entailed aristocratic sympathies.

The leader of the Mountain and the true statesman of the Revolution was Robespierre. The period of his reign represented the highest achievement of the Revolution. "Robespierre inaugurated a policy which was at once national and democratic. At the very outset of his effort, he had to struggle, even in Paris, against the extremists of the left, allied to the extremists of the right. He had, furthermore, to give them battle at a moment when the famine had grown worse and when disastrous news from the frontiers was piling up. That he did not despair, that he accepted power at such a moment, that he carried so crushing a burden without weakening, and that he succeeded in rescuing the Republic from the abyss should be sufficient for his fame."[15]

Danton, whom Aulard had considered the great figure of the Revolution, was only an opportunist, a man who sought to patch out expedients without principle or scruple, an adventurer with no sincere devotion to the Republic.[16] The high repute of Danton and his followers was incorrectly attributed to them by later generations, for their true character was so well known to their contemporaries that their deaths caused no emotion at the time, and even the Thermidorean Convention refused to rehabilitate them.[17]

Since the struggle between the Gironde and the Mountain had been more than political, the victory of the Mountain had more than political consequences. The system of economic intervention which culminated in the Ventôse decrees took on the character of a social revolution. "It was no longer a matter of momentarily restraining a hostile party by force. The question was one of dispossessing it forever, crushing it in its means of existence, and raising to social life, by means of its spoils, the class of the eternally disinherited. . . . The Terror was no longer ashamed of itself. It was becoming an established order, a red crucible where future democracy was being forged from the accumulated ruins of all that belonged to the old regime."[18] The social regime which the Terror set up was never consolidated, however. Its purposes were not understood by those who were to have benefited from it and, in truth, the actual effect of the measures taken was to produce distress for many of the common people.[19]

The defeat which the Terror sustained fundamentally transformed the character of the Republic and began the recession of the Revolution. "A product of the war and its sufferings, the Republic was forcibly cast in the mill of the Terror, against its principles; it was really, in spite of its prodigies, only an accident. Supported on an increasingly narrow base, it was never understood by the very people it wanted to bring into a share in its life. It required all the ardent mysticism of its authors and their superhuman energy to make it last up to the point of victory abroad. Twenty centuries of monarchy and bondage are not wiped out in a few months. The most rigorous laws do not have the power to change human nature and the social order with a single blow. Robespierre, Couthon, Saint-Just, who wanted to prolong the dictatorship in order to create new civil institutions and to over-throw the empire of wealth, knew this well. They could have succeeded only if they had controlled the whole dictatorship in their own hands. But the intransigence of Robespierre, who broke with his colleagues in the government just at the moment when they were making concessions to him, was enough to bring down an edifice suspended in the void of laws. A memorable example of the limits of the human will when it comes to grips with the resistance of material things."[20]

The degradation of the Revolution which followed the fall of Robespierre was implicit in the nature of the forces which brought it about. "The Ninth of Thermidor resulted from a coalition between the Plain, which had been passive up to this point, and all the remnants of the former Dantonist party, allied for the moment with the majority of the governmental committees. The motivating element of that coalition was made up of the old friends of Danton, . . . of all the corrupt former proconsuls, sullied by crimes and plunderings, whom Robespierre had recalled from their missions and attempted to bring to an accounting. These unscrupulous men of affairs, in order to save their heads, had succeeded in setting the Plain in motion by promising to oppose the application of the Ventôse laws, which were striking at the life and property of the suspects as a group. The Plain had finally given over Robespierre for fear of his social policy."[21]

The regime which followed was one of systematic corruption. "The great period of the Republic ended all at once. Personal rivalries took precedence over ideas; Public Safety faded away, or disappeared behind private interests or hatreds and passions. The politician re-placed the man of policy. All the statesmen were dead. Their suc-cessors, who sharply disputed with one another for power, were incapable of forming stable majorities about their meager persons. Their momentary successes never had a future. They upset one another and gave themselves over to the most astounding mutual outbiddings, to the most sudden about-faces, to the most degrading reversals, in order to bring success to their petty enterprises, at the expense of the country, if need be. Everything inauspicious, dissolvent, and corrupting which the parliamentary regimes bear within themselves when they are not quickened and curbed by the moral discipline of leaders worthy to command and by the vigilance of an informed and organized opinion, calculated selfishness, in short, suddenly broke out. . . . The private and collective interest of the deputies was scandalously opposed to the national interest."[22]

The people might have risen again to restore the Republic of the Mountain, but the leaders of the popular party did not measure up to their opportunities. The deputies of the Mountain hesitated, waiting on a tenuous legality, while the people drifted purposelessly. "So, as often happens, the democratic forces were of better stuff than their leaders. Those artisans, starved for months, who were ready to revolt and throw themselves against the police and the army of order, were of a different temper from the deputies who disavowed in advance any suspicion of accord with insurrection. The deputies of the Mountain, in spite of the sincerity of their feelings, were nevertheless of a different class from the people. They had all sprung from the bourgeoisie and could understand the people only by an intellectual effort. They were not on an even ground with the manual laborers, from whom they were separated by education, fortune, and family prejudices. . . . The men of the Mountain defended the people by procuration. But before the people could conduct their affairs by themselves, before they even learned to read, almost a century would pass."[23]

The interpretation of the Revolution which Mathiez offered followed substantially the pattern of Jaurès's earlier work. Its socialist tendency was not so explicit, however. Mathiez, a professional historian, confined himself more closely to the narrative of events than did Jaurès, who, as an active political leader, was immediately concerned with the bearing of the historical event on problems of current political conflict.

Both agreed with the republicans that the Revolution was the product of circumstances, not of abstract theory. They defined these circumstances in terms of the material basis of society in production relations. The Revolution was the work of the advancing bourgeoisie and was progressive because the bourgeoisie, in virtue of the objective circumstances of that historic moment, was the bearer of progress. The Revolutionary affirmation of democracy and the equal rights of men was a lasting work. But changed historic conditions were to render inadequate the particular form in which the bourgeoisie had expressed these ideas and to impose on a new class the task of maintaining the Revolution by extending it.

The Republic under the Terror, and especially during Robespierre's reign, foreshadowed the manner in which this would one day be done. As the men who represented the highest development of the Revolution conceived its mission, it meant a gigantic effort to raise those social classes which have been "eternally disinherited." The scope of this task far surpasses any sort of palliation or adjustment within a framework which presupposes that society will always be divided into superiors and inferiors. The Revolution would be fulfilled only as a consequence of the accession of a new class to power, not simply through taxation nor any such superficial measures as those which Aulard and the republicans would offer.

The contrast which Mathiez set into relief between the Republic of the Terror and the Republic after Thermidor could hardly fail to suggest a broader contrast, that between the Republic as it once had been and must be again, and the actual Third Republic of the twentieth century, the "oligarchy of politicians, the *République des camarades.*"[24]

Such a presentation of the events of the Revolution, as it was taken up by a socialist and communist left, became part of the criticism of the existing Republic and a definition of what Liberty, Equality, and Fraternity should mean for the generation which had just passed through the World War. In the analysis of the Revolution, as in contemporary France, the left gave full credit to the bourgeois republicans when they stood with the common people in struggle against the right. But the left denounced the bourgeois republicans when they grew fearful of their special class interests and tried to set up barriers against the popular forces.

The conservative viewpoint was sustained during the post-War years in the history of the Revolution published by Pierre Gaxotte. Gaxotte did not present his work as the product of fresh research: his interpretation depended on Taine and Cochin, and he made large use of Mathiez's works, in support of opposite conclusions. Historical writings of considerable substance, related to the Revolutionary period, were published by other conservatives during these years; among such were the studies of corporate institutions under the old monarchy for which Olivier-Martin was responsible, and the works of Jacques Bainville, the outstanding historian of the *Action française*. But Gaxotte's volume was the only general account of the Revolution to be presented in behalf of the right, and it attained a wide audience.

The old order of France was not unattractive, as Gaxotte viewed it. "The France of the *ancien régime* was a very great and very old edifice, which had been built by fifty generations, stretching back through more than fifteen centuries. They had each left a mark on it, always adding to what remained from earlier times, and scarcely ever removing or tearing down any of it. So its plan was confused, the styles disparate, the rooms irregular. Some abandoned parts were threatened with ruin; others were inconvenient; others, too luxurious. But, taken all in all, it had an imposing air, and more people lived there in a better fashion than anywhere else."[25]

This old France was in a sound condition in respect to its economy, but it was encountering difficulty in its financial system.[26] The country was rich and its wealth increasing. It was the state that was poor, because of an ineffective tax system and a lack of control over expenditure. "Pre-Revolutionary France was not at all unfortunate. It had occasion to complain, but not to revolt. Of the two great problems which were imposed on public attention, financial reform and the

abolition of the vestiges of feudalism, neither would have been in-
soluble if an intellectual and moral crisis had not struck the French
soul to its depths."[27]

The revolutionary spirit was the factor which made the crisis
desperate. The revolutionary idea was supported by the growth of
science, even though it was not itself scientific.[28] Science offered no
verification of the doctrines from which the Revolution issued, but
it did give support to a contempt for the past which made those
principles receive a readier hearing.

The revolutionary doctrines received their force from the organization created about them in the *sociétés de pensée*. "The supporters
of the new theories in the eighteenth century did not remain isolated.
They formed associations to pool their knowledge and sum up their
ideas. That organization became apparent in 1720, and it gained
ground rapidly in 1750. At the death of Louis XV, it was fully developed. Associations of fine wits and hearty intellects multiplied in
every town—literary salons, academies, reading rooms, patriotic
societies, schools, museums, Masonic lodges, agricultural societies.
They held sessions at regular intervals. There the members read and
above all, held discussions. A whole army of thinkers entered into
controversy and deliberated on the questions of the day: the grain
trade, new taxes, provincial assemblies, or on problems of doctrine:
the role of civilization, natural rights, the fundamentals of society."[29]

The conditions inherent in the nature of these clubs were such as
to render the faults of the revolutionary doctrines more grievous. The
life of the societies was entirely different from real life. "In life, to
govern means to struggle against material things, to foresee, prepare,
organize, act; here [in the societies], the great art consists of drawing
up the agenda and securing a majority. In life, a thought is judged by
experience, by the test of facts. Here, opinion reigns, what secures the
assent of the listeners is real, what obtains their adherence is true. In
life, man is not an isolated individual but part of the social organism;
he is a member of a family, of a professional body; he is guided by all
sorts of considerations which do not belong in the domain of verbal
logic: religion, faith, morals, tradition, sentiment, political loyalty,

professional duty. In the *société de pensée,* the initiate wipes away all that is not abstraction and speculative reason. He discards all that is truly personal; he reduces himself to that little deductive faculty which is the most common thing in the world."[30]

The first steps towards meeting the crisis of the state were taken by the monarchy. But at almost every turn the Court succeeded only in weakening its own position, not in accomplishing reform. The halting, confused, hesitant policy of the monarchy reduced France to effective anarchy.

This opened the way for the conquest of power by the clubs. "From the deputies whose election they had secured, they received regular communications. As these were printed, posted up, discussed, and circulated in every manner, they oriented opinion and exposed, truly or falsely, the intentions of the Court, the dangers which threatened Liberty, the measures which the capital had already taken and which were required of the provinces, if they wished to show themselves its equals in patriotism."[31]

The Revolution progressed naturally from the Constituent to the Convention: there was no abrupt shift of policy between one stage and another. "Superficial observers sometimes oppose . . . [the work of the Constituent] to that of the other two Assemblies. This is sheer fantasy. The policy of the Constituent so profoundly committed the future that the Legislative and the Convention could scarcely do other than to submit to or develop its effects. There was neither division nor deviation between them, but an insensible succession. What one did, the other had prepared."[32]

The force of circumstances tends to vindicate the royalists more than it does the revolutionaries.[33] The attack on the throne is not to be justified on the ground that the King had gone over to the counter-revolution. But his recourse to the emigration is to be understood as a natural reaction after the Assembly had interfered in his religious life by forcing him to assent to the Civil Constitution. The war was decided on by the revolutionists for their own purposes. The insurrection of August, 1792 and the execution of the King were deliberately chosen policies, aimed at putting a clear division between the forces of the Revolution and those who were not wholeheartedly in sympathy with it.

Within the Convention, the Girondins represented no sounder tendency than did the Mountain; they simply favored an impossible attempt to endorse the principles which were the source of the Revolution and still hold back their inevitable consequences. The Girondins were republican, democratic, anticlerical. But they wanted a government which would be withdrawn from the influence of the rabble, freed from insurrections and the power of the *faubourg Saint-Antoine*. They wanted to say: the Revolution halts where we stand. "The Revolution would come to a halt one day, indeed, but only when it had developed its principles to their final limits. We are not yet there. The parliamentary radicalism of the Girondins was only a step towards the dictatorial communism which appeared among the men of the Mountain."[34]

The communism which the Mountain represented was the true outcome of the Revolution. But "to that communism, too precise outlines must not be given, nor too completely finished formulas. It was an elementary communism, an almost instinctive rising of the poor against the rich, of have-nots against haves."[35] As living conditions grew worse, communism gained ground. The leaders of the Mountain did not avow their adherence to it, but what they refused to concede as a system, they granted piecemeal. Many influences bore on this result. The extreme left, the *Enragés,* who openly advocated communism, were stealing support from Robespierre, Marat, and the established chiefs of the left. Economic necessity reinforced the tactical consideration, for the financial instability caused by the *assignat* inflation was severely afflicting those who supported the Revolution, and the *laisser faire* policy of the Girondins afforded no relief. Beyond that, the socialist argument of the *Enragés* was supported by the logic of the revolutionary doctrines. "A formal and deductive spirit like Robespierre's could not remain insensible to this compulsion. Even while he manifested great distrust and even aversion for the *Enragés,* he would be led by the progress of his reflection as much as by the pressure of the working classes to adopt, piece by piece, the whole program of the *Enragés*. He would impose it on the Convention and he would succumb in trying to impose it on the country."[36]

The Terror was not halted until after men, goods, ideas, and religion had all been thrown into the melting pot.[37] The overthrow of Robespierre and the end of the communist Terror was not accomplished by men who, more than he, had the public good in mind. The Thermidoreans performed their function in their own interests, for reasons of personal rivalry. But their work happened to coincide with a necessary stage in the deliverance of the nation. Once they had checked the Revolution, the true France was able to assert its right to a measure of decency.

The Directory in no wise returned to sound principles. It was a regime of trimming, conducted by hypocrites. The revolutionists who had surrounded Robespierre had at least been sincere; their successors carried on much of the Terror but lacked even that virtue. All that remained to them of the revolutionary ardor was the determination to destroy the Church. "The men of the Directory persecuted priests only in order to strike at religion. While they served their own interests, they were also doctrinaires, and they were the more attached to their doctrines because, through them, they avoided the secret contempt of their own thoughts. They had no illusions about the life they led, nor the regime they created, nor the people of whom they made use. But, in the mire in which they were being engulfed, they held on to something of a fragmentary ideal. To liberate the human spirit, to establish a rational morality, was a bit of the revolutionary dream. In serving it, they affirmed their fidelity to their youth, they posed as theorists and philosophers. Let them be treated as sectaries, *illuminés,* fanatics— that is what they wanted. Perhaps then it would be forgotten that they were corrupt.[38]

From this sorry state, the Revolution passed into the hands of Bonaparte, who saved as much of it as possible.[39] It was the ultimate fate of the doctrinaires of the Revolutionary period, who set out to regenerate humanity and remake the world, to entrust themselves to a general in order to avoid recalling the Bourbons.

The Revolution thus appeared much the same to Gaxotte as it had to Taine, his precursor by some four or five decades. Although there were grave defects in the old order, the revolutionary movement did not arise from them. Cochin had explicitly denied, in fact, there was a need or a necessity for the Revolution. The upheaval was the consequence of a body of doctrines, put into practice by a determined band of men. Its principles afforded no stopping place, once they were granted, until the Revolution had run its full term. Its course was governed by the laws of development of the *sociétés de pensée*. The *sociétés* were the directing force which perfected the ideas of the Revolution, organized the united support of a group behind them, and controlled their operation.

The outcome of the revolutionary process was the destruction of religion, property, family, individual personality: it was the end of decent society.

The conservative account of the Revolution, as it was presented by Gaxotte, continued to run parallel to the social politics of the right. Gaxotte avoided dealing directly with the rights of democratic government; he did not endorse the political power of the people, but neither did he make a frontal attack on the popular classes. He pointed his opposition to the expression of democratic government in the bureaucratic republic; he sharply contrasted the multiform state of the old monarchy with the uniform, omnipresent state of his own day, personified in the eternal and immutable functionary seated behind a grilled window.[46] This was the point on which the right focussed its attention in its criticism of the Third Republic.

Gaxotte's picture of the culmination of the Revolution in communism was quite the same outcome which the right feared from the development of the Third Republic, which claimed to be its heir. Nor would the conservatives of the times, mindful of the disciplined power of the Communist and Socialist parties, find it hard to appreciate the dominant role of the political clubs in turning the Revolution towards communism. Just as the right and the extreme left had much in common in their criticism of the Republic, so was Gaxotte able to make use of Mathiez's studies. He agreed with Mathiez in regard to the socialist nature of the high period of the Revolution and in his contempt for the bourgeois republic which followed it.

Finally, Gaxotte was not able, more than the politicians of the right, to formulate a positive alternative to the Revolution which he condemned.

Although a large number of the historical scholars of the generation following the World War, probably the preponderant number, held to a republican viewpoint, none of them published a history of the Revolution comparable to Aulard's. The two important republican histories of the Revolution to appear in these years were both co-operative works, published as volumes in historical series. The collaborators were professional historians who had made an intensive study of the Revolutionary period, but none of them had found occasion to present a general synthesis independently. One of these volumes was written by Georges Lefebvre, Raymond Guyot, and Philippe Sagnac.[41] The other work was published by Philippe Sagnac and Georges Pariset.[42] Both accounts restated the republican analysis with little divergence from the established form.

The source of the Revolution still seemed to Lefebvre, who was responsible for the main part of the study on which Guyot and Sagnac also collaborated, to be in the material circumstances of the times. The intellectual progress of the eighteenth century had undermined the authority of princes and churches, but "a more powerful force, still unrecognized, was sapping the old edifice—modern capitalism. This originated in England, thanks to the industrial revolution; it was already being instituted in France, and the whole world was eventually to submit to its laws. But, in assuring preponderance to the bourgeoisie, it was to bring economic and civil liberty to all quarters, along with the constitutional regime and the abolition of privileges."[43]

The process of the Revolution was a steady adjustment to circumstances: the hostile maneuvers of the Court, the nobles, and the Church. Such exigencies justified the declaration of war on the coalition" and the widening perspectives of the measures taken against the Church." In such a manner, the Revolution moved through its early stages to the great crisis in the period of the Convention.

The development of the Revolution at this stage was governed by the struggle between the Gironde and the Mountain.

The political principles of the Gironde favored democracy as the natural fulfillment of the Revolution, but the party was so much bound to the wealthy middle class that it lost its effectiveness as a leader of the revolutionary movement. The Girondins had only a distant sympathy for the people, while they readily accepted the support of the bourgeois who grouped themselves behind the party. The divergence between the Gironde and the common people was revealed in the conflict between the economic liberalism of the Gironde and the interventionism which the representatives of the people demanded."

The Mountain was quite as bourgeois in its leadership, but it retained a direct contact with the common people and thereby learned that, if the Revolution were to succeed, some satisfaction must be given to the need of the people for measures to protect its means of livelihood." The willingness to yield to popular demands was the factor which allowed the Mountain to secure leadership of the Convention. The liberalism of the Girondins could not meet the requirements of the nation at war, and they could not win a successful conclusion to the war which they had themselves precipitated."

The social policy of the Mountain was equivocal, however, and its original ambiguity accounted in large part for the fate of its policy. The Terror, which gave expression to the program of the Mountain, was essentially a response to circumstances, and it combined a policy of national defense with elements of a social revolution." This confusion derived from the fact that the war itself was both national and social. "The Third Estate was not only defending the soil of the fatherland; it was prosecuting a struggle against the aristocracy that had begun in 1789. It had seen part of its members, rich and poor, pass over to the enemy; but the *sans-culottes* were only the more ardent to finish the extermination of the opposing class and all those who had passed over to it."[50]

The Mountain therefore sanctioned a policy of national control over wealth. This exceeded the limits of interventionism and, with the Ventôse decrees, approached socialism.[51] But the intention of the Mountain was not socialist: it was nationalist. The program was a deception, for the Jacobins turned the intervention to the account of the state, which they controlled, rather than to the benefit of the people themselves.[52]

This deception proved only temporarily successful. The revolutionary government did not succeed in binding the rural proletariat to its cause, and the illusory assistance given to the *sans-culottes* of the cities did not bring a firm support. From both a political and a social viewpoint, therefore, the leaders of the Mountain eventually found themselves suspended in a void.[53] When, in the midst of the economic crisis, the chiefs of the Terror fell out among themselves, the deep-seated opposition of the bourgeoisie was able to assert itself and bring the Terror to a halt.[54]

The Convention, in spite of its ultimate fate, carried forward the work of the National Assembly and left an ineffacable mark on the heritage of the Revolution.[55] It founded political democracy as well as the rule of the middle class; the instruments of government it worked out proved a precedent for political development during the nineteenth century. The leaders of the Mountain especially made a lasting contribution in establishing that "the state had the right and duty of intervening to correct social inequality, either by limiting great fortunes through means of progressive taxation and inheritance laws, or by protecting the poor from wretchedness by the proclamation of the right to work, the control of prices of commodities of prime necessity, the distribution of generous public relief, and the sale of lands at low prices. With the aid of circumstances, they nationalized a notable part of economic activity. What would they have kept of their work once the crisis were passed? No one knows. Still, they did create an interventionist or *étatiste* tradition which is at the root of French 'radicalism.' "[56] In the same manner, the Mountain fixed other elements into the republican tradition: hostility to the Roman church, and the doctrine of natural frontiers.

The government of the Directory was marked by the lack of youth and genius, but not of good intentions; its failure was due as much to the difficulties of the situation as to the policies of the responsible figures. "The republican government seems to have been sincere in wishing to make France richer than the monarchy had left it—or to make it so again. With the exception of some individuals, always the same ones, few of the men were intent on the establishment of their own fortunes at any price, over the ruins of the state and the public. The personal ambition of the middle bourgeois was real but modest, and the majority only wanted to acquire or keep a house and garden for their old age. They were, at heart, sensibly more ambitious for their country than for themselves."[57] The corruption of society, which has been so prominently featured in histories of the period, was insignificant: it was not peculiar to the Directory and was remarkable only in contrast to the Spartan republic of the Year II.[58]

The men of the Directory failed "for lack of the genius and the youth which was necessary. But perhaps the time was not yet ripe. Bonaparte, who had youth and genius, would perhaps not have had better success if he had taken power in the Year IV."[59] When Bonaparte did take power, after the Directory had shown its inability to maintain a middle way, he only followed in the footsteps of his predecessors, but with better fortune. "The 18th of Brumaire was, in principle, only a last effort towards that *juste milieu* that had been attempted by a minority of parvenus of the Revolution, now supported by a general need for order and peace and by the 'connivance of fluid capital.'"[60]

This interpretation did not depart in fundamentals from the republican pattern. The Revolution was a system of expedients, yet it discovered principles of lasting value. These include political democracy, nationalism, and an anticlerical rationalism. Aulard's judgment, generally supporting the Revolutionary war, was followed rather than that of the extreme left. The social program of the Terror was the foundation of state intervention to maintain justice among social classes, rather than a foreshadowing of the socialist effort to use state power for the purpose of destroying the basis for the existence of classes.

The work on which Philippe Sagnac and George Pariset collaborated also followed the conventions of the republican school.

After a narration of the origins of the Revolution which featured the role of circumstances, the achievements of the National Assembly were reviewed. "How could so considerable a work, the greatest that men ever performed, be realized, and so quickly? It was because the Assembly had been animated by a profound enthusiasm and an infinite love for the public welfare; it bore within itself the high ideal of liberty and justice; its reforms had been prepared by the intellectual and political work of a whole century. It followed the general movement of public opinion; it legislated, in a way, under the dictate of a Nation which had previously expressed its wishes in the *Cahiers* and which put forth new and stronger ones in its assemblies and clubs. The People, that of the Bastille and the Federation, permitted the Assembly to rise above itself and gave it the will and the force to accomplish everything."[61]

The Legislative carried on the work of the National Assembly. It properly responded to the needs of the situation by declaring war on the coalition and was sufficiently successful in it to make possible the establishment of a Republic in the midst of monarchical Europe.[62] It strengthened the laic and anticlerical spirit. It affirmed political equality and furthered republicanism.

The conflict between moderates and democrats which occupied the Convention "was not solely political, but social as well. *Culottes dorées* and *sans-culottes*. The rich and the well off were not Girondins, yet the Girondins bore the weight of an alliance which they had not sought and which, besides, had failed them."[63] The struggle of parties became one of classes: the bourgeoisie against the people.

The two great figures of the Convention, Danton and Robespierre, were equally patriotic.[64] Danton's policy put the unity of the revolutionary forces as the prime need of France. Robespierre argued that the rupture among the revolutionaries was a fact which could not be remedied, and that mercy towards those who were weak in their allegiance to the Revolution would simply deliver the movement into their unsteady hands; the only recourse was to a frankly dictatorial government, built on the recognition that the party of the Revolution was a minority and must be maintained by force. Of these two policies, that proposed by Robespierre was the sounder. Danton endangered the whole of the Revolution, for in his efforts to sustain unity, he could not guarantee even that France would have any government. Robespierre's program was the only one that could mobilize patriotic fervor within the army and thereby save France.

But the government of the Terror, which finally accepted Robespierre's conception, depended for its survival on conditions that did not obtain for long. The chief of these were the submission of the country, the support of the Convention, and the unity of the leaders of the government.[65] It was inevitable, however, that the leaders should eventually clash, and when their disagreement became open, the entire structure of government was doomed.

The Directory, which the victors of Themidor set up, could be called either a system of balance or a system of seesaw.[66] It was an effort to attain a middle course. But it failed to find strength enough for effective government, and it was swept away by Bonaparte.

This interpretation, like the other republican account, followed a familiar pattern. The latter presentation showed deviations under the influence of Mathiez. But the analysis by Sagnac and Pariset departed from that by Aulard in giving less attention to social implications and being more preoccupied with political developments. The republican historians as a group did not pass beyond the limits of the older republican conventions. As with Aulard, so with them, the Revolution was an adjustment to circumstances which also embodied principles of lasting truth: political democracy, anticlericalism, nationalism. The significance of the Revolution as a source of a policy of state intervention for social reform, which had been introduced in Aulard's generation, had now become an integral part of the republican presentation.

In all this the republican historians continued to conform with the republican politicians. They, too, were carrying on a definition of the

Revolutionary heritage which dated from the generation before the first World War—a policy of democratic republicanism and of social reform through state action, but within the framework of capitalism.

In another respect, something of a parallel appeared between the contemporary situation and that presented by the republican historians. The Directory had generally received an unfavorable judgment from the historians who dealt with it. The conservatives viewed it as a degenerate form of the Revolution, and the republicans regularly emphasized the responsibility it bore for the rise of Bonaparte.[67] During the two decades following the War, the conservative Gaxotte had viewed it as the continuation of the Terror under the control of hypocrites, instead of zealots; Mathiez had considered it the prototype of corrupt parliamentarism. But the republican historians of this generation did not join in the condemnation. Pariset did not clearly vindicate the Directory, but he gave no noteworthy criticism of it. Guyot presented it as ineffective, but took pains to point out that the motives and character of the responsible men of the time were not blameworthy.

The correspondence is apparent between the situation of the republicans of the Directory, attempting to pursue a middle course between Jacobinism and Royalism, and the republicans of the Third Republic, beset at once by a conservative opposition that was hostile to the Republic and a socialist left that gave it a revolutionary meaning. The circumstances of the twentieth century would make it easier for the republicans to view with charitable sympathy the position of their predecessors at the very end of the eighteenth century.

CHAPTER SIX

CONCLUSION

THE MAIN OUTLINE of the conservative interpretation of the Revolution underwent little change during the Third Republic.[1] The core of the Revolution remained what it had been for Taine: a work of ideas, of reform conceived in abstract terms, in disregard for tradition, in illusory imitation of science. The whole revolutionary idea was built on a mistaken view of man as an isolated atom, uniform with all his fellows. The preoccupation with politics implied a definition of man as a creature living only in the state, and the state as the only institution by which he might express himself. The consequence of this doctrine was the destruction of all the mediating institutions by which real men live and develop, the Church, the family, and private property, which makes it possible for men to maintain their autonomy.

This presentation of the Revolution conformed particularly with the social experience of the aristocratic right of Taine's day. For the established families of landed wealth, life was stable, governed by tradition, and it afforded little incentive or occasion for sudden change or innovation. Men of such a background found their chief values in a multiplicity of institutions, among which the state played only a small part. Although such a way of life was characteristic of the country gentry, its conditions did not differ greatly from those of many an urban family of long-established fortune. The commercial or banking family was common in which wealth and a way of living firmly ordered by unchanging conventions passed from one generation to another. It was taken for granted that only an aristocratic minority would enjoy the full benefits of such a station. But those less favored would find an honorable place in the proper fulfillment of their functions in the social hierarchy, and relief in the Christian charity and solidarity which binds all classes.

This way of life was deeply transformed with the acceleration of the industrial revolution in France at the end of the nineteenth century. The great growth of industry so increased the power of urban wealth that there was no longer question of maintaining a balance: landed wealth became an appendage of modern capitalism. The process was furthered by the wider use of devices for the mobilization of capital, divorced from management responsibility. At the same time, the rise of proletarian socialism, an unwelcome addition to the forces of re-publicanism, steadily pressed on the bourgeoisie which had been the core of the republican parties, and many of its members passed into alliance with elements which had been identified with opposition to the Republic.

This development was reflected in the conservative account of the Revolution. The older viewpoint, which had been presented by Taine, was not discarded. The charge of the conservatives that the Revolution tended naturally to socialism was apparently strengthened by the rise of effective socialist party organization. But as the masses came in-creasingly to participate in current political life, the conservative presentation of the role of the people in the Revolution altered. Where Taine had violently condemned the popular risings in support of the Revolution, Cochin was concerned with the laws by which popu-lar sovereignty deceives the people. His approach had the effect of relieving the people of the responsibility for the Revolution and pre-sented them as dupes of the professional politicians who inevitably seize control of sovereignty whenever it is formally invested in the people.

This redirection of the conservative position, achieved early in the twentieth century, gave it the form which it retained through the end of the Third Republic. The Revolution now appeared as a body of doctrines which, under the *sociétés de pensée,* tend to eventuate in the full socialization of life. This negative analysis, which rejected the *ancien régime* together with the Revolutionary epoch and its heritage, did not receive a programmatic formulation even down to the end of the Republic.

The republican account of the Revolution, as it stood at the beginning of the Third Republic, explained the events of the revolutionary period as the natural reaction of reasonable men to the need for reform implicit in the circumstances of the old regime.[2] These include political democracy, nationalism, and the narrowing of the area in which the Church may hold sway over the nation. The Revolution formed one continuous whole and, once it had begun its course, it proceeded inevitably to the form which it reached under the Convention. From the confusion of this period, there emerged the full expression of the movement: the democratic republic.

The republican historians wrote as much in accordance with their social experience as did the conservatives. Their histories formed part of the ideology of a bourgeoisie which was enterprising, innovating, self-confident. Its position as the leading element in the nation, it took as a matter of course. It supported political democracy without hesitating for fear that this would result in a challenge to its authority. It advanced nationalism as the proper binding element in society. If it was not frankly materialist, it was certainly secular. All of the values it cherished could be fully satisfied in the course of day-to-day life in a world of competitive business.

The state was a center of the social philosophy of the republican bourgeoisie, but it was not therefore given a wide scope of action. Its intervention in the economy was settled by parliamentary empiricism rather than by general theory. There was no considerable republican opinion during the early decades of the Republic which held that the state has a general duty to intervene in the workings of society in order to produce social equality or to redress economic disparities.

The shift in French life which took place near the turn of the century had a more severe effect on the historical work of the left than it did on that of the right. Not only was the republican interpretation modified, but a new socialist school branched from it and asserted an independent position. The socialists stood with the republicans in opposition to the right: to the same extent, they subscribed as well to the specific expression of the Revolution in the democratic republic, popular nationalism, and anticlericalism.

But the socialist historians, like the socialist party leaders, held themselves apart from their allies. They considered the Revolution a work of the bourgeoisie which, while progressive in its historic context, bore the limiting marks of the class which had been its author. The achievement of political democracy, which was its mission, depended largely on the steady support and impetus supplied to the middle class by the common people. This popular force carried the Revolution forward to a point beyond the bounds which the bourgeoisie had set to it. The regime of the Terror meant the use of state power to effect a social revolution which would establish true equality and virtue.

Just so, the socialists in contemporary life sought to extend the Republic beyond the limits sanctioned by their republican allies. Like the Jacobins, they called on the people to defend the democratic republic, because the middle class could not be trusted to do this of itself. Even in endorsing the heritage of the Revolution, the socialists assigned their own meanings to the republican creed of democracy, nationalism, and laicity. For the socialists, democracy meant the actual participation of the people in political life and the conduct of state policy in the interests of the working class, considered as the representative of the whole people. The use of national interest to conceal the purposes of the bourgeoisie as a class was repudiated in socialist theory. The conflict with the Church was not simply directed against a political opponent: it was part of the struggle to destroy the hold of religious faith over men's lives.

The divergence of the socialist interpretation from the main stream of republican thought modified the course of the historical controversy. The republicans, in meeting this new critique, did not basically alter the position they had inherited from an earlier generation. But they did come to see in the Terror an attempt to secure social equality by the use of state power, though within the framework of capitalist property; and this figured as the historical precedent for the interventionist social politics of the republicans in the twentieth century.

The work of the historians in the generation following the World War continued within the outline of the pre-War tendencies. The adjustments which had earlier been made, from left to right, were sufficient for the period after the War.[3] The attack on the Directory from the two flanks and the sympathy which the republicans showed for its endeavor only emphasized the centrist position into which republicanism had been moving for some time.

The course of historical writing on the Revolution during the Third Republic indicates that the problem of the causes of the Revolution, its nature and significance, involved much more than an academic controversy waged only by professional historians and with only the resources of archival research. The interpretation of the Revolution was generally understood to hold a meaning for contemporary life, and assumed forms which were in consonance with the chief bodies of opinion on social politics. Both the views of the historians on the Revolution and the outlook of Frenchmen on the state of their nation showed reflections of the same forces, and were modified in parallel fashion when social experience and the conditions of social life underwent change.

The conflicting judgments on Revolutionary history expressed the division of social forces in France and the cleavage in thought on the proper form of state and society. The viewpoint on the historical problem defined the position of the two nations, the France of the Revolution and the France of the Counterrevolution. It revealed as well the separate life of socialist France, within and beside the France of the republican Revolutionary heritage.

As a reflection of social forces the historical interpretation of the Revolution played an important role throughout the Third Republic. The crises about the constitutional issue, which marked the first generation of the Republic, were largely acute expressions of differences summed up in the evaluation of the Revolutionary legacy. The separation of tendencies to the right and left of the republican in the analysis of Revolutionary history manifested in one way the clearer polarization of social forces on either side of republicanism which marked French life after the World War. The nature of the regime which eventually displaced the Republic is perhaps also suggested by the development of the historical controversy.

The seventy years of historical study of the Revolution during the Third Republic did not produce agreement on the crucial points of the problem. Indeed, there was even less when the Republic was brought to an end than there had been when it was founded, for a socialist interpretation had appeared which would have been rejected by both of the antagonists who held the field at the beginning of the period.

This disunity persisted and extended in spite of a profusion of monographic research. The importance attached to the historical problem by contemporaries of all opinions produced a thorough and full study of the materials on the Revolutionary history; both governmental and private resources were generously devoted to the work. This detailed research opened up new ranges of material and brought increasing certainty on positive fact, on those points of information that could be discovered and verified without room for question.

But the progress of research did not solve the problem of interpretation. Social experience and social forces operating within the Third Republic continued to shape the contradictory tendencies of historical judgment.

The study of the process by which historical opinion on the Revolution was conditioned by current social politics during the Third Republic sets into relief a problem for which it does not supply the answer: if the interpretation of the Revolution has been determined by contemporary forces rather than by historical materials, what then is its validity? Such a question can scarcely be ignored, but since it is part of the whole problem of the nature and value of history, for which the historiography of the Revolution serves as only one relevant example, it can not be considered adequately here. So fundamental a question can not be treated properly as an appendix to the present investigation. No more can be offered than suggestions of a few possible answers.

One response to the problem is to reject the whole effort to supply synthesis and interpretation to history, to abandon the idea of causation and assume an indifference to the outcome of historic developments. Or it is possible to view historical knowledge as relative and conditional, rather than absolute and objective, and to defend it on that basis. In this way, any interpretation can be considered valid for those who believe it; or usefulness instead of truth can be taken as the test to apply to historical judgment. But such views of the soundness of historical interpretation would not fully satisfy those men who sought in the history of the Revolution a reliable assistance in coping with the current problems of France.

But it is also possible to recognize the manner in which men's conceptions of history are conditioned, and still to find in history a trustworthy guide for action in the present. Even though historical interpretation is shaped by patterns of social thinking, it does not necessarily follow that it is impossible to arrive at objective truth. That men have disagreed on the significance of the Revolution does not imply that their conflicting judgments are all false, nor that there is only a subjective "truth." It is scarcely unusual in history for propositions indubitably false to be widely or universally believed, and the reasons for their general credence are frequently commonplace historical knowledge, the Ptolemaic theory, for example. Such a circumstance does not make it necessary to re-examine them or to hesitate in pronouncing them false. Truth and general credence are distinct matters. This study has dealt with the history of beliefs about the Revolution: it does not preclude a separate study of the development of certain knowledge of even the controversial problems of the Revolution, nor does it imply that it is impossible to choose among conflicting interpretations on the basis of their truth.

There is good reason to suggest that historical truths eventually gain general acceptance, and that judgments of the Revolution will, in the long run, approach agreement. The diverging opinions on the Revolution depend on general social philosophies, but these social philosophies themselves submit to a test in reality. General judgments on the nature and position of mankind in society have varying fortunes: they survive and die, they wax and wane. It can reasonably be contended that their fate is related to the degree in which they are based on fact, to the extent to which they correspond to reality. Such a proving of social philosophies is, as well, a trial for the interpretations of historical events which they condition. The interpretation is thereby tested in history, rather than in historiography.

Such a position bears implications for the historian who would properly fulfill his function. If the product of historical study is tested by social life as well as by the canons of historical research, the data supplied by present-day life are as pertinent to the work of the historian as those data which remain from past events.

Historical study can thus serve its purpose the better for a recognition that it is an inseparable part of the life of its times.

NOTES

I: HISTORY AS PRESENT POLITICS

1. That historical interpretation of the Revolution has reflected contemporary social views is rather obvious to anyone who has dealt with the literature of the Revolution, but the precise nature of the relationship has not received much direct study. Most reviews of historical writing on the Revolution have been in the nature of critical bibliographies; their concern has been with the development of historical knowledge of the Revolution and the soundness of arguments in support of one or another contention. The course of historical judgment on the Revolution has been treated in a few works, some of the more important of which will be cited at the appropriate places later in this work; but attention has been directed to the individual historians rather than to the social influences controlling the life of an interpretation considered as a social fact. Two brief essays by contemporary American scholars suggest the approach which is used in this study, but neither develops the material from the present viewpoint. One of these is by Louis R. Gottschalk, "The French Revolution: Conspiracy or Circumstance?," included in a volume of essays in honor of George Lincoln Burr entitled *Persecution or Liberty* (New York, 1931), pp. 445–72. The other is the bibliographical essay by Crane Brinton in his *A Decade of Revolution: 1789–1799* (3d ed., New York, 1934), pp. 293–302. A three-volume work on the historiography of the French Revolution by N. Kareiev, published in Leningrad in 1924, enjoys good repute but, since it has not been translated from the original Russian, it is not generally available and could not be utilized for the present study.

II: BEFORE THE THIRD REPUBLIC

1. The literature on the history of France in the nineteenth century leaves much to be desired. Historical writing in the field has been concerned primarily with problems of governmental policy and with the succession of constitutional and political crises. The long-term developments in French life have not been studied directly to any important extent; they have been treated incidentally to the consideration of shorter-term developments in political history. But the approach dictated by the

history of political regimes is frequently inappropriate to the study of secular movements, and the latter have therefore never received adequate study. Specific references can not be supplied, consequently, for many of the generalized observations of French social history which are offered in the course of the present study; they have been gleaned from a number of works which are not directly pertinent. In the course of the chapters which deal with the period of the Third Republic, indication will be made of the works which are most useful for the history of social politics in those times. But in connection with the present chapter on the half-century preceding the Third Republic, mention may be made of a few books dealing with long-term movements in nineteenth-century France. Two important works on economic history go far towards filling the deficiency of the ordinary political histories. They are J. H. Clapham, *The Economic Development of France and Germany: 1815–1914* (Cambridge, 1921) and S. B. Clough, *France: A History of National Economics: 1789–1939* (New York, 1939). A. L. Guérard passed beyond conventional limitations in his *French Civilization in the Nineteenth Century: A Historical Introduction* (New York, 1914), but the work does not pretend to be a thorough examination. R. H. Soltau, *French Political Thought in the Nineteenth Century* (New Haven, 1931), covers an important field throughout the century. The brief essay by Godfrey Elton on *The Revolutionary Idea in France: 1789–1871* (London, 1923), gives promise of a fresh approach, but actually contributes nothing new, either in material or in analysis. *Revolution and Reaction in Modern France,* by G. Lowes Dickinson (London, 1892), covers the same period, 1789–1871, and is likewise concerned with the continuing progress of the struggle for and against the principles of the Revolution; but it adds nothing to the conventional political histories and, moreover, has been outdated some time.

2. This point is developed further at the beginning of Chapter Four.

3. Brief discussions of the historians of the Revolution who published during the years under consideration here may be found in G. P. Gooch, *History and Historians in the Nineteenth Century* (2d ed., London, 1913); Lord Acton, *Lectures on the French Revolution* (London, 1910); and P. Janet, *Philosophie de la Révolution française* (4th ed., Paris, 1892).

4. Baronne de Staël-Holstein, *Considérations sur les principaux événemens de la Révolution française* (3 vols., Paris, 1818).

5. L. A. Thiers, *Histoire de la Révolution française* (1st ed., 10 vols., Paris, 1823–1827; 13th ed., 10 vols., Paris, 1870–1872).

6. F. A. Mignet, *Histoire de la Révolution française depuis 1789 jusqu'en 1814* (1st ed., Paris, 1824; 9th ed., 2 vols., Paris, 1865).

7. P. J. B. Buchez and P. C. Roux, *Histoire parlementaire de la Révolu-*

tion française, ou journal des assemblées nationales depuis 1789 jusqu'en 1815 (40 vols., Paris, 1834–1838).

8. François Droz, *Histoire de la Révolution française* (3 vols., Paris, 1839–1842).

9. Alphonse de Lamartine, *Histoire des Girondins* (1st ed., 8 vols., Paris, 1847; 4th ed., 4 vols., Paris, 1848).

10. Louis Blanc, *Histoire de la Révolution française* (1st ed., 12 vols., Paris, 1847–1862; also, 15 vols., Paris, 1878).

11. Jules Michelet, *Histoire de la Révolution française* (1st ed., 7 vols., Paris, 1847–1853; also, 9 vols., Paris, 1877–1878).

12. Alexis de Tocqueville, *L'Ancien Régime et la Révolution française* (1st ed., Paris, 1853; also, 2 vols., Paris, 1856).

13. Edgar Quinet, *La Révolution* (1st ed., Paris, 1856; also, 2 vols., Paris, 1868).

III: DURING THE STRUGGLE ABOUT
THE REPUBLIC

1. The development of social forces and social politics during the Third Republic, which forms a large part of the present study through its reflection in historical judgment on the Revolution, has never received adequate direct treatment. It has been considered incidentally in a number of works organized primarily about other points of interest. This aspect of the present study rests, therefore, on a number of works to which specific citations can not be given, inasmuch as they do not bear directly on the subject. The works which have been helpful, in greater or lesser degree, will be indicated. But the literature on the social history of France under the Republic has not been exhaustively examined in the preparation of this work, and the references do not purport to be a complete bibliography. Fuller discussions of historical writing on the Third Republic may be found elsewhere; two good bibliographies are those by R. A. Winnacker, in his "Bibliographical Article: The Third French Republic: 1870–1914," published in the *Journal of Modern History*, X (1938), 372–409, and by S. B. Clough, in the notes to his book *France: A History of National Economics: 1789–1939*, pp. 444–87. The Third Republic has received a number of sound and recent treatments, but they generally suffer from a preoccupation with political history, in its narrow sense. Two modern works have appeared in English: D. W. Brogan; *France under the Republic: The Development of Modern France, 1870–1939* (New York, 1941); and R.W. Hale, Jr., *Democratic France: The Third Repub-*

lic from Sedan to Vichy (New York, 1941). One of the best studies is contained in the two volumes by Charles Seignobos, *Le Déclin de l'Empire et l'établissement de la Troisième République: 1859–1875*, and *L'Evolution de la Troisième République*, which appeared as Vols. VII and VIII of the series edited by Ernest Lavisse under the title *Histoire de France contemporaine depuis la Révolution jusqu' à la paix de 1919* (Paris, 1921). The usual republican tendency can be corrected by consulting John Labusquière, *La Troisième République: 1871–1900*, Vol. XII of *Histoire socialiste: 1789–1900*, edited by Jean Jaurès; Alexandre Zévaès, *Histoire de la Troisième République: 1870–1926* (Paris, 1926), socialist; Jean Galtier-Boissière *et al., Histoire de la Troisième République* (Paris, 1935), written under the influence of the *Front populaire;* Jacques Bainville, *The French Republic: 1870–1935* (translated by Hamish Miles, London, 1936), a study by a prominent member of the royalist *Action française.* Other general histories, useful in some degree, include Emile Bourgeois, *History of Modern France,* two vols. in *Cambridge Historical Series:* Vol. II, 1852–1913 (Cambridge, 1919); J. C. Bracq, *France under the Republic* (New York, 1916); P. de Coubertin, *The Evolution of France under the Republic* (translated by I. F. Hapgood, New York, 1897); Michel Lhéritier, *La France depuis 1870* (Paris, 1922); Maxime Petit *et al., Histoire de France: La Troisième République* (Paris, 1936); Raymond Recouly, *The Third Republic,* in series *The National History of France,* edited by F. Funck-Brentano (translated by E. F. Buckley, London, 1928); Fritz Roepke, *Von Gambetta bis Clemenceau: fünfzig Jahre französischer Politik und Geschichte* (Stuttgart and Berlin, 1922). An important contribution is made in Pierre de Pressac, *Les Forces historiques de la France: la tradition dans l'orientation politique des provinces* (Paris, 1928); R. H. Soltau, *French Parties and Politics: 1871–1921* (London, 1922), is a useful manual. Charles W. Pipkin's *Social Politics and Modern Democracies,* 2 vols.: Vol. II (New York, 1931), does not do full justice to its title.

2. Gabriel Hanotaux, *Contemporary France* (English translation, 4 vols., London, 1903–1909), covering the years from 1870 to 1882, is one of the fullest accounts of parliamentary affairs during the early Republic. A broader but superficial treatment of the same period is Daniel Halévy, *La Fin des notables* (2 vols., Paris, 1930–1937). More detailed works on particular aspects of the period include F. H. Brabant, *The Beginnings of the Third Republic in France: A History of the National Assembly, February–September, 1871* (New York, 1940); Maurice Deslandres, *Histoire constitutionnelle de la France: l'avènement de la Troisième République: la Constitution de 1875* (Paris, 1937); André Bellesort, *Les Intellectuels et l'avènement de la Troisième République: 1871–1875* (Paris, 1931). Two

important articles on the significance of the elections during the early Republic are R. A. Winnacker, "The French Election of 1871," *Papers of the Michigan Academy of Science, Arts and Letters*, XXII (1938), 473–83; and A. Lajusan, "Les Origines de la Troisième République: 'quelques éclaircissements, 1871–1876," *Revue d'histoire moderne*, V (1930), 419–38. Among the biographical studies of use are J. M. S. Allison, *Monsieur Thiers* (London, 1932); Ernst Lewinsky, *Thiers und der Pakt von Bordeaux* (Berlin, 1927); Paul Deschanel, *Gambetta* (London, 1920); H. M. Hyndman, *Clemenceau: The Man and His Times* (New York, 1919).

3. Among the works on the *Seize-Mai* are M. de Marcère, *Le Seize-mai et la fin du septennat* (Paris, 1900); Maurice Reclus, *Le Seize-mai* (Paris, 1931); and Alexandre Zévaès, *Au Temps du Seize-mai* (Paris, 1932).

4. One of the best accounts of the Boulangist period is Adrien Dansette, *Le Boulangisme: 1886–1890* (Paris, 1938). Material of some value may be found in Alexandre Zévaès, *Au Temps du Boulangisme* (5th ed., Paris, 1930). Felix Challeton's *Cent Ans d'élections: histoire électorale et parlementaire de la France de 1789 à 1890* purports to be a three volume history of France; as such, it is trifling. But the last two volumes (Paris, 1891), which are largely given over to the Boulangist campaigns, contain a number of the manifestoes of the time and much illuminating detail.

5. Dansette's volume on Boulangism was to be completed with a study of the Dreyfus affair; the work would fill a needed gap, but apparently has not yet appeared. The standard work is Joseph Reinach, *Histoire de l'affaire Dreyfus* (7 vols., Paris, 1901–1911).

6. *The History of the Commune of 1871* by P. O. Lissagaray (translated by E. M. Aveling, London, 1886), has a quality which later historians have not surpassed. A good recent account is Frank Jellinek, *The Paris Commune of 1871* (London, 1937). E. S. Mason, *The Paris Commune: An Episode in the History of the Socialist Movement* (New York, 1930), contains material on the controversy over the significance of the Commune. Other accounts are Thomas March, *History of the Paris Commune of 1871* (London, 1896); and John Leighton, *Paris under the Commune* (London, 1871). A detailed study, dealing chiefly with the administration of justice, is Georges Laronze, *Histoire de la Commune de 1871, d'après des documents et des souvenirs inédits: la justice* (Paris, 1928).

7. Charles Chesnelong, *Un Témoignage sur un point d'histoire: la campagne monarchique d'octobre 1873* (Paris, 1895).

8. H. A. Taine, *Les Origines de la France contemporaine: L'Ancien Régime* (1st ed., Paris, 1875; 16th ed., Paris, 1891).

9. H. A. Taine, *Les Origines de la France contemporaine: La Révolu-*

tion (1st ed., 3 vols., Paris, 1878–1884; Vol. I, 16th ed., Paris, 1888; Vol. II, 10th ed., Paris, 1884; Vol. III, 8th ed., Paris, 1885).

10. Taine, *L'Ancien Régime*, pp. 3–110.

11. *Ibid.*, pp. 11–220.

12. *Ibid.*, p. 215.

13. *Ibid.*, pp. 221–328.

14. *Ibid.*, pp. 399–428.

15. *Ibid.*, pp. 440 f.

16. Taine, *La Révolution*, I, 66.

17. *Ibid.*, II, 34–36.

18. *Ibid.*, I, 388 ff.

19. *Ibid.*, II, 141 ff.

20. *Ibid.*, II, 64.

21. *Ibid.*, II, 470–71.

22. *Ibid.*, III, 78–109.

23. *Ibid.*, I, 386.

24. *Ibid.*, III, 629.

25. *Ibid.*, III, 635; also III, 590–635.

26. *Ibid.*, I, 179 f.

27. *Ibid.*, III, 132 ff.

28. An especially valuable work, although it is limited to political theory, is Charlotte T. Muret, *French Royalist Doctrines since the Revolution* (New York, 1933). General tendencies in the right during this period are suggested in P. T. Moon's *The Labor Problem and the Social Catholic Movement in France: A Study in the History of Social Politics* (New York, 1921).

29. Georges Avenel, *Lundis révolutionnaires, 1871–1874: nouveaux, éclaircissements sur la Révolution française à propos des travaux les plus récents et des faits politiques contemporains* (Paris, 1875); Marcellin Pellet, *Variétés révolutionnaires* (3 vols., Paris, 1885–1890); Eugène Spuller, *Hommes et choses de la Révolution* (Paris, 1896).

30. Avenel, *op. cit.*, p. 65.

31. *Ibid.*, pp. 160–72; see also Pellet, *op. cit.*, I, 143 ff., 233, 242.

32. Avenel, *op. cit.*, pp. 147–48.

33. See, for example, *ibid.*, pp. 36 f., 47 f., 177.

34. Spuller, *op. cit.*, p. 10.

35. Avenel, *op. cit.*, p. 94

36. Spuller, *op. cit.*, p. 68.

37. See, for example, Pellet, *op. cit.*, II, 165 ff.

38. *Ibid.*, I, 350 f., 358; Avenel, *op. cit.*, pp. 140, 220–35.

39. Avenel, *op. cit.*, pp. i–ii, 60, 140; Pellet, *op. cit.*, II, 10.

40. See, for example, on the right, Paul Baudry, *La Révolution française: 1789–1799* (Rouen, 1890); Gaston Feugère, *La Révolution française et la critique contemporaine* (Paris, 1889); Charles d'Héricault, *La France révolutionnaire: 1789–1889* (Paris, 1889); and on the left, Edmé Champion, *L'Esprit de la Révolution française* (Paris, 1887); E. Guillon, *Histoire de la Révolution et de l'Empire* (Paris, 1892); Paul Janet, *Histoire de la Révolution française* (Paris, 1889).

41. Albert Sorel, *L'Europe et la Révolution française* (8 vols., Paris, 1885–1904).

42. Sorel, *Révolution française,* Vol. I (4th ed., Paris, 1897), 537–38.

43. *Ibid.,* I, 538.

44. Sorel, *Révolution française,* Vol. II (3d ed., Paris, 1897), 265.

45. Sorel, *Révolution française,* Vol. IV (3d ed., Paris, 1898), 452.

46. *Ibid.,* IV, 449, and passim.

47. *Ibid.,* I, 540.

48. *Ibid.,* II, 521–22; see also, for similar passages, II, 109; III, 414.

49. *Ibid.,* II, 527–34, 565 f.; III, 539 ff.

50. *Ibid.,* IV, 122 ff.

51. *Ibid.,* IV, 470 and passim.

52. *Ibid.,* I, passim: especially pp. 1–8, 185, 201 ff., 240 f.

IV: UNDER THE IMPERIAL REPUBLIC

1. Beyond the general works on the history of the Republic, of which the most useful have been cited earlier, little is available specifically dealing with the period just before the first World War. Interpretive suggestions may be found in the relevant passages of C. J. H. Hayes, *A Generation of Materialism: 1871–1900,* a volume in the *Rise of Modern Europe* series, edited by W. L. Langer. Important material is also supplied by J. H. Clapham, *The Economic Development of France and Germany: 1815–1914,* chs. viii, ix, x, xii, xiii; and S. B. Clough, *France: A History of National Economics: 1789–1939,* ch. vii.

2. The best studies of the economic development of modern France are those by Clapham and Clough. Material on the business cycle may be found in W. L. Thorp, *Business Annals* (New York, 1926); Albert Aftalion, *Les Crises périodiques de surproduction* (2 vols., Paris, 1913); Lucien March, "Le Mouvement des prix et l'activité productrice," *Bulletin de la Statistique générale de la France,* Vol. I (1911). The *résumé rétrospectif* tables in the *Annuaire statistique,* published by the *Ministère du travail et la prévoyance sociale: bureau de la Statistique générale,* are a ready reference for the most important data. Reviews of business condi-

tions were published each week in the *Economiste français*, beginning in April, 1873.

3. On the history of the labor movement during the Third Republic, the second volume of Edouard Dolléans, *Histoire de mouvement ouvrier: 1830–1939* (2 vols., Paris, 1939), has replaced the two more or less standard works which have been long out-dated: Emile Levasseur, *Questions ouvrières et industrielles sous la Troisième République* (Paris, 1907); and Georges Weill, *Histoire du mouvement social en France: 1852–1902* (Paris, 1904). Paul Louis, *Histoire de la classe ouvrière en France de la Révolution à nos jours: la condition matérielle des travailleurs, les salaires, et la coût de la vie* (Paris, 1927), has some advantages over the earlier studies, but is far from adequate. Among the best histories of the socialist parties during the Republic is Alexandre Zévaès, *Le Socialisme en France depuis 1871* (Paris, 1908); Paul Louis, *Histoire du parti socialiste en France: 1871–1914* (Paris, 1922); and Daniel Halévy, *Essais sur le mouvement ouvrier en France* (Paris, 1901) are of some value. Léon Blum, *Les Congrès ouvriers et socialistes français* (2 vols., Paris, 1901), is of great assistance in following out the party conflicts and schisms during the 1880s. Several of the studies in a series edited by Alexandre Zévaès under the title *Histoire des partis socialistes en France* are helpful: among them are two by Zévaès himself, *Les Guesdistes* (Paris, 1911); and *De la Semaine sanglante au Congrès de Marseilles: 1871–1879* (Paris, 1911); and Jacques Prolo, *Les Anarchistes* (Paris, 1912). An earlier study of comparable sort is A. Zévaès, *Aperçu historique sur le Parti ouvrier français* (Lille, 1899). Among the studies of the early years of the labor movement are Samuel Bernstein, *The Beginnings of Marxian Socialism in France* (New York, 1933); M. R. Kelso, "The Inception of the Modern French Labor Movement, 1871–1879: A Reappraisal," *Journal of Modern History*, VIII, (1936), 173–93; and Samuel Bernstein, "Jules Guesde, Pioneer of Marxism in France," *Science and Society*, IV (1940), 29–56. Jaurès, the dominating figure in the socialist movement just before the War, has received biographical treatment in H. R. Weinstein, *Jean Jaurès: A Study of Patriotism in the French Socialist Movement* (New York, 1936); Weinstein's views may be compared to those of Samuel Bernstein in "Jean Jaurès and the Problem of War," *Science and Society*, IV (1940), 127–64. The history of the labor movement as a whole can be understood better by the use of Jürgen Kuczynski, *Labour Conditions in Western Europe: 1820–1935,* (New York, 1937).

4. The rise of syndicalism is treated in the course of several of the works on the labor movement cited earlier. It has received direct consideration in Louis Lorwin, *Syndicalism in France* (New York, 1914).

5. On developments in royalist political theory, see C. T. Muret, *French Royalist Doctrines,* especially chs. x–xv.

6. Aulard's contribution to historical study of the Revolution is discussed in an essay by James L. Godfrey which appears as chapter iii in a volume of historiographical studies edited by B. E. Schmitt, *Some Historians of Modern Europe* (Chicago, 1942).

7. Alphonse Aulard, *Histoire politique de la Révolution française: origines et développement de la démocratie et de la république: 1789–1804* (Paris, 1901).

8. *Ibid.,* p. vi.

9. *Ibid.,* p. 28.

10. This and the two previous quotations are from *ibid.,* p. 46.

11. *Ibid.,* pp. 112, 153.

12. *Ibid.,* pp. 179, 278.

13. *Ibid.,* p. 358.

14. *Ibid.,* pp. 466–93.

15. *Ibid.,* pp. 49 f., 367 ff., 459, 521.

16. *Ibid.,* p. 521.

17. *Ibid.,* p. 418.

18. *Ibid.,* p. 423.

19. *Ibid.,* pp. 424 f.

20. *Ibid.,* pp. 494 ff., 521.

21. *Ibid.,* pp. 571 f., 690.

22. *Ibid.,* pp. vii, 425.

23. *Ibid.,* p. 782.

24. *Ibid.,* p. 46.

25. *Ibid.,* p. 47.

26. Louis Madelin, *La Révolution,* in *Histoire de France racontée à tous,* edited by F. Funck-Brentano (1st ed., Paris, 1911; 5th ed., Paris, 1914), pp. 557–58.

27. *Ibid.,* p. 14.

28. *Ibid.,* p. 558

29. *Ibid.,* p. 558.

30. *Ibid.,* p. 558.

31. *Ibid.,* pp. 559–60.

32. *Ibid.,* pp. 559–60.

33. *Ibid.,* pp. 559–62.

34. This and the preceding quotation are from *ibid.,* p. 562.

35. *Ibid.,* pp. 387, 395.

36. *Ibid.,* pp. 406, 563.

37. *Ibid.,* p. 266, for example.

38. Jean Jaurès, Vols. I–V of *Histoire socialiste, 1789–1900,* edited by Jean Jaurès (Paris, 1901–1905).

39. *Ibid.,* I, 3.

40. *Ibid.,* I, 7–8.

41. *Ibid.,* I, 38; also pp. 32 ff.

42. *Ibid.,* I, 302.

43. *Ibid.,* I, 396–97.

44. *Ibid.,* I, 606 ff.

45. *Ibid.,* II, 1312.

46. *Ibid.,* II, 837.

47. *Ibid.,* II, 917, 1312.

48. *Ibid.,* II, 796 ff., 837 ff.

49. *Ibid.,* II, 837 f.

50. *Ibid.,* II, 891 ff.

51. *Ibid.,* II, 1286–87.

52. *Ibid.,* IV, 1458 ff.

53. *Ibid.,* IV, 1769 ff.

54. *Ibid.,* IV, 1799 ff.

55. *Ibid.,* IV, 1811. — The suceeding volume in the series in which Jaurès's work appeared continued the account as far as the Consulate. The analysis of the period is definitely hostile to the regime which succeeded the Convention.

56. *Ibid.,* I, 533; see also, I, 24.

57. Alphonse Aulard, *Taine: historien de la Révolution française* (1st ed., Paris, 1907; 2d ed., Paris, 1908).

58. Augustin Cochin, *La Crise de l'histoire révolutionnaire: Taine et M. Aulard* (1st ed., Paris, 1909; 2d ed., Paris, 1909).

59. *Ibid.,* p. 33.

60. *Ibid.,* p. 35.

61. *Ibid.,* p. 36. — The *Confédération générale du travail (C.G.T.),* the federation of trade unions, was especially active at the time.

62. *Ibid.,* p. 37.

63. *Ibid.,* p. 43.

64. *Ibid.,* pp. 47 ff.

65. *Ibid.,* p. 51.

66. *Ibid.,* pp. 51 ff.

67. Augustin Cochin, *La Révolution et la libre-pensée: la socialisation de la pensée, 1750–1789; la socialisation de la personne, 1789–1792; la socialisation des biens, 1793–1794* (first published c. 1910. Paris, 1924), pp. 172–73.

68. Augustin Cochin, *Les Sociétés de pensée et la démocratie: études*

d'histoire révolutionnaire (1st ed., Paris, c. 1910; 2d ed., Paris, 1921), pp. 235 ff.

69. *Ibid.*, pp. 157 ff., 203, 219.
70. Cochin, *Révolution,* passim.
71. *Ibid.*, p. 241.
72. Cochin, *Sociétés,* p. 288.
73. *Ibid.*, pp. 290 ff.
74. Cochin, *Révolution,* p. 248.

V: AS THE REPUBLIC GREW OLDER

1. There is no adequate treatment of the history of France between the first World War and the second, for obvious reasons. The period is covered briefly in two histories of the Third Republic which appeared after 1939: D. W. Brogan, *France under the Republic: The Development of Modern France, 1870–1939,* and R. W. Hale, Jr., *Democratic France: The Third Republic from Sedan to Vichy.* Much material of fundamental importance is included in S. B. Clough, *France: A History of National Economics: 1789– 1939.* The *Social and Economic Studies of Post-War France,* edited by C. J. H. Hayes, are a series of works of real substance, but they cover the period only to the late 1920s. Among the volumes of most use in the present connection are C. J. H. Hayes, *France, A Nation of Patriots* (New York, 1930); W. F. Ogburn and William Jaffé, *The Economic Development of Post-War France: A Survey of Production* (New York, 1929); and David Saposs, *The Labor Movement in Post-War France* (New York, 1931).

2. Mathiez's career as an historian and his relations with Aulard are discussed in an essay by Frances Acomb which appears as ch. xiv in *Some Historians of Modern Europe.* References to other literature on the subject are given in the footnotes to the study.

3. Albert Mathiez, *La Révolution française* (1st ed., 3 vols., Paris, 1922– 1927; Vol. I, 4th ed., Paris, 1930; Vol. II, 3d ed., Paris, 1929; Vol. III, 3d ed., Paris 1930).

4. *Ibid.,* I, 1.
5. *Ibid.,* I, 47.
6. This and the preceding quotations are from *ibid,* I, 77.
7. *Ibid.,* I, 123.
8. *Ibid.,* I, 145.
9. *Ibid.,* I, 158.
10. *Ibid.,* II, 168 ff.—See also *ibid.,* I, 186 ff.
11. *Ibid.,* II, 169.
12. *Ibid.,* II, 3.

13. *Ibid.,* II, 69.
14. *Ibid.,* III, 12–13.
15. *Ibid.,* III, 25.
16. See, for example, *ibid.,* II, 43.
17. *Ibid.,* III, 165.
18. *Ibid.,* III, 149.
19. *Ibid.,* III, 149, 171 ff.
20. *Ibid.,* III, 223.
21. Albert Mathiez, *La Réaction thermidorienne* (Paris, 1929), pp. 4–5. This work, according to the author's preface, "succeeds the summary in three volumes . . . entitled *La Révolution française."*
22. *Ibid.,* p. 3.
23. *Ibid.,* p. 258.
24. A characterization of the Directory: *ibid.,* p. 282.
25. Pierre Gaxotte, *La Révolution française* (Paris, 1928), p. 7.
26. *Ibid.,* pp. 28–41, 47 f.
27. *Ibid.,* p. 48.
28. *Ibid.,* pp. 57 f.
29. *Ibid.,* p. 63.
30. *Ibid.,* pp. 64–65.
31. *Ibid.,* p. 124
32. *Ibid.,* pp. 165–66.
33. *Ibid.,* pp. 179, 206–22, 242 ff., 264 ff.
34. *Ibid.,* p. 259 and *supra.*
35. *Ibid.,* p. 259.
36. *Ibid.,* pp. 261–62.
37. *Ibid.,* p. 381 ff.
38. *Ibid.,* p. 425.
39. *Ibid.,* p. 446.
40. *Ibid.,* pp. 14 ff.
41. Georges Lefebvre, Raymond Guyot, Philippe Sagnac, *La Révolution française* (Paris, 1930), Vol. XIII of the series *Peuples et civilisations: histoire générale,* edited by Louis Halphen and Philippe Sagnac.
42. Philippe Sagnac, *La Révolution: 1789–1792* (Paris, 1920); Georges Pariset, *La Révolution: 1792–1799* (Paris, 1920): Vols. I and II of *Histoire de la France contemporaine depuis la Révolution jusqu'à la paix de 1919,* edited by Ernest Lavisse.
43. Lefebvre, *op. cit.,* p. 1.
44. *Ibid.,* p. 105, for example.
45. *Ibid.,* pp. 61 ff.
46. *Ibid.,* pp. 101, 118, 146.

47. Lefebvre, *op. cit.*, pp. 201 ff., 232 f., 247 ff.

48. Lefebvre felt that the Gironde was not impolitic in seeking the war. The fault was in the way it prosecuted the war. *Ibid.*, p. 105.

49. *Ibid.*, pp. 127, 199, 232 f.

50. *Ibid.*, p. 233.

51. *Ibid.*, pp. 241–48.

52. *Ibid.*, p. 233.

53. *Ibid.*, pp. 233, 247 f.

54. *Ibid.*, pp. 253, 264 ff.

55. *Ibid.*, pp. 281 f.

56. *Ibid.*, p. 282.—The portion of the history which treats of the Directory was written by Raymond Guyot.

57. *Ibid.*, pp. 317–18.

58. *Ibid.*, p. 312.

59. *Ibid.*, p. 307.

60. *Ibid.*, p. 441.

61. Lavisse (ed.), *op. cit.*, I, 330.

62. *Ibid.*, I, 351 f., 435 f.

63. *Ibid.*, II, 93.

64. *Ibid.*, II, 162 ff.

65. *Ibid.*, II, 235 ff.

66. *Ibid.*, II, 299.

67. There were historians, of course, including republicans, who had looked on the Directory with favor in earlier periods. See, for example, E. Guillon, *Histoire de la Révolution et de l'Empire*, pp. 167 f. But opinion generally was adverse.

VI: CONCLUSION

1. Although a considerable body of opinion hostile to the Revolution long antedates the Third Republic, no historical account which entirely rejected the Revolutionary movement and its tradition had gained wide influence, comparable to that of Taine's study, before the time of the Third Republic. This suggests the question of whether the strength of the counter-revolutionary historiography from the early years of the Republic onwards reflects a significant turn of opinion in contemporary social politics after the events of 1870–1871. But the available evidence is not adequate to determine whether or not this was actually the situation.

2. The names, "conspiracy thesis" and "circumstance thesis," which Cochin gave to the two opposing interpretations and which have had some currency since his time, serve well as short titles, but are open to miscon-

struction. Each school recognized that both ideas and conditions contributed to the outbreak of the Revolution. But the conservatives held that its primary source was the spirit of Revolutionary reform, and it was merely aided in its progress by the circumstances of the old society. The republicans insisted that the Revolution was essentially an effort to meet an objective need for reform, although the reform was necessary because of the contradiction between facts and those ideas of justice, reason, and equality which are the lasting heritage of the Revolution.

3. The growth of corporative doctrines on the right in the post-War years was parallelled in historical writing by conservatives which gave a more favorable treatment to corporate institutions under the old monarchy. These studies accorded well with the conventional interpretation of the right, which commonly expressed its opposition to the Revolution by criticizing it for destroying mediating institutions and giving place only to individuals and to the state. But this material was not embodied in a general historical account of the Revolution.

BIBLIOGRAPHY

SELECTED WORKS ON THE HISTORY OF THE
FRENCH REVOLUTION

Aulard, Alphonse, Histoire politique de la Révolution française: origines et développement de la démocratie et de la république: 1789–1804. Paris, 1901.

——— Taine: historien de la Révolution française. 1st ed., Paris, 1907. 2d ed., Paris, 1908.

Avenel, Georges, Lundis révolutionnaires, 1871–1874: nouveaux éclaircissements sur la Révolution française à propos des travaux les plus récents et des faits politiques contemporains. Paris, 1875.

Baudry, Paul, La Révolution française: 1789–1799. Rouen, 1890.

Blanc, Louis, Histoire de la Révolution française. 1st ed., 12 vols., Paris, 1847–1862. Also, 15 vols., Paris, 1878.

Buchez, P. J. B., and P. C. Roux, Histoire parlementaire de la Révolution française, ou journal des assemblées nationales depuis 1789 jusqu'en 1815. 40 vols., Paris, 1834–1838.

Champion, Edmé, L'Esprit de la Révolution française. Paris, 1887.

Cochin, Augustin, La Crise de l'histoire révolutionnaire: Taine et M. Aulard. 1st ed., Paris, 1909. 2d ed., Paris, 1909.

——— La Révolution et la libre-pensée: la socialisation de la pensée, 1750–1789; la socialisation de la personne, 1789–1792; la socialisation des biens, 1793–1794. First published about 1910. Paris, 1924.

——— Les Sociétés de pensée et la démocratie: études d'histoire révolutionnaire. 1st ed., Paris, c. 1910. 2d ed., Paris, 1921.

Droz, François, Histoire de la Révolution française. 3 vols., Paris, 1839–1842.

Feugère, Gaston, La Révolution française et la critique contemporaine. Paris, 1889.

Gaxotte, Pierre, La Révolution française. Paris, 1928.

Guillon, E., Histoire de la Révolution et de l'Empire. Paris, 1892.

Héricault, Charles d', La France révolutionnaire: 1789–1889. Paris, 1889.

Janet, Paul, Histoire de la Révolution française. Paris, 1889.

Jaurès, Jean, Vols. I–IV of Histoire socialiste, 1789–1900, ed. by Jean Jaurès. Paris, 1901–1905. Vol. I, La Constituante: 1789–1791. Vol. II, La Législative: 1791–1792. Vol. III, La Convention (I): la République; les idées politiques et sociales de l'Europe et de la Révolution: 1792. Vol. IV, La Convention (II): la mort du roi; la chute des Girondins; idées sociales de la Convention; gouvernement révolutionnaire; 1793–1794 (9 thermidor).

Lamartine, Alphonse de, Histoire des Girondins. 1st ed., 8 vols., Paris, 1847. 4th ed., 4 vols., Paris, 1848.

Lefebvre, Georges, Raymond Guyot, Philippe Sagnac, La Révolution française. Vol. XIII of Peuples et civilisations: histoire générale, ed. by Louis Halphen and Philippe Sagnac. Paris, 1930.

Madelin, Louis, La Révolution. In series L'Histoire de France racontée à tous, ed. by F. Funck-Brentano. 1st ed., Paris, 1911. 5th ed., Paris, 1914.

Mathiez, Albert, La Réaction thermidorienne. Paris, 1929.

Mathiez, Albert, La Révolution française. 1st ed., 3 vols., Paris, 1922–1927. Vol. I, La Chute de la royauté: 1787–1792, 4th ed., Paris, 1930. Vol. II, La Gironde et la Montagne, 3d ed., Paris, 1929. Vol. III, La Terreur, 3d ed., Paris, 1930.

Michelet, Jules, Histoire de la Révolution française. 1st ed., 7 vols., Paris, 1847–1853. Also, 9 vols., Paris, 1877–1878.

Mignet, F. A., Histoire de la Révolution française depuis 1789 jusqu'en 1814. 1st ed., Paris, 1824. 9th ed., 2 vols., Paris, 1865.

Pariset, Georges, La Révolution: 1792–1799. Vol. II of Histoire de France contemporaine depuis la Révolution jusqu'à la paix de 1919, ed. by Ernest Lavisse. Paris, 1920.

Pellet, Marcellin, Variétés révolutionnaires. 3 vols., Paris, 1885–1890.

Quinet, Edgar, La Révolution. 1st ed., Paris, 1856. Also, 2 vols., Paris, 1868.

Sagnac, Philippe, La Révolution: 1789–1792. Vol. I of Histoire de France contemporaine depuis la Révolution jusqu'à la paix de 1919, ed. by Ernest Lavisse. Paris, 1920.

Sorel, Albert, L'Europe et la Révolution française. 1st ed., 8 vols., Paris, 1885–1904. Vol. I, Les Moeurs politiques et les traditions, 4th ed., Paris, 1897. Vol. II, La Chute de la royauté, 4th ed., Paris, 1897. Vol. III, La Guerre aux rois, 1792–1793, 3d ed., Paris, 1897. Vol. IV, Les Limites naturelles, 1794–1795, 3d ed., Paris, 1898. Vol. V, Bonaparte et le Directoire, 1795–1799, 1st ed., Paris, 1903.

Spuller, Eugène, Hommes et choses de la Révolution. Paris, 1896.

Staël-Holstein, Baronne de, Considérations sur les principaux événemens de la Révolution française. 3 vols., Paris, 1818.

Taine, H. A., Les Origines de la France contemporaine. 1st ed., 6 vols., Paris, 1875–1894. L'Ancien Régime, 16th ed., Paris, 1891. La Révolution: I, L'Anarchie, 16th ed., Paris, 1888. La Révolution: II, La Conquête jacobine, 10th ed., Paris, 1884. La Révolution: III, Le Gouvernement révolutionnaire, 8th ed., Paris, 1885.

Thiers, L. A., Histoire de la Révolution française. 1st ed., 10 vols., Paris, 1823–1827. 13th ed., 10 vols., Paris, 1870–1872.

Tocqueville, Alexis de, L'Ancien Régime et la Révolution française. 1st ed., Paris, 1853. Also, 2 vols., Paris, 1868.

SELECTED WORKS ON THE HISTORY OF FRANCE

DURING THE THIRD REPUBLIC [1]

Acomb, Frances, "Albert Mathiez (1874–1932)," in B. E. Schmitt, ed., Some Historians of Modern Europe: Essays in Historiography by Former Students of the Department of History of the University of Chicago, Chicago, 1942, pp. 306–24.

Acton, Lord, Lectures on the French Revolution. Ed. by J. N. Figgis and R. V. Laurence. London, 1910.

Aftalion, Albert, Les Crises périodiques de surproduction. 2 vols., Paris, 1913.

Allison, John M. S., Monsieur Thiers. London, 1932.

Annuaire statistique. Published annually by République française: Ministère du travail et de la prévoyance sociale: Statistique générale.

Bainville, Jacques, The French Republic: 1870–1935. Trans. by Hamish Miles. London, 1936.

Bellesort, André, Les Intellectuels et l'avènement de la Troisième République: 1871–1875. Paris, 1931.

Bernstein, Samuel, The Beginnings of Marxian Socialism in France. New York, 1933.

—— "Jean Jaurès and the Problem of War," *Science and Society,* IV (1940), 127–64.

—— "Jules Guesde, Pioneer of Marxism in France," *Science and Society,* IV (1940), 29–56.

Blum, Léon, Les Congrès ouvriers et socialistes français. 2 vols., Paris, 1901.

Bourgeois, Émile, History of Modern France. 2 vols., Vol. II: Cambridge, 1919. In Cambridge Historical Series.

Brabant, Frank Herbert, The Beginnings of the Third Republic in France: A History of the National Assembly, February–September, 1871. New York, 1940.

Bracq, Jean Charlemagne, France under the Republic. New York, 1916.

Brinton, Crane, A Decade of Revolution: 1789–1799. 3d ed., New York, 1934. In The Rise of Modern Europe series, ed. by W. L. Langer.

---

[1] Including also works on the historiography of the Revolution.

Brogan, D. W., France under the Republic: The Development of Modern France, 1870–1939. New York, 1941.

Challeton, Félix, Cent Ans d'élections: histoire électorale et parlementaire de la France de 1789 à 1890. 3 vols., Vols. II and III: Paris, 1891.

Chesnelong, Charles, Un Témoignage sur un point d'histoire: la campagne monarchique d'octobre 1873. Paris, 1895.

Clapham, J. H., The Economic Development of France and Germany: 1815–1914. Cambridge, 1921.

Clough, Shepard B., France: A History of National Economics: 1789–1939. New York, 1939.

Coubertin, Pierre de, The Evolution of France under the Republic. Trans. by Isabel F. Hapgood. New York, 1897.

Dansette, Adrien, Le Boulangisme: 1886–1890. Paris, 1938.

Deschanel, Paul, Gambetta. London, 1920.

Deslandres, Maurice, Histoire constitutionnelle de la France: l'avènement de la Troisième République: la Constitution de 1875. Paris, 1937.

Dickinson, G. Lowes, Revolution and Reaction in Modern France. London, 1892.

Dolléans, Edouard, Histoire du mouvement ouvrier: 1830–1939. 2 vols., Paris, 1939.

Economiste français. Published weekly at Paris, beginning April 19, 1873.

Elton, Godfrey, The Revolutionary Idea in France: 1789–1871. London, 1923.

Galtier-Boissière, Jean, with the collaboration of Réné Lefebvre, Michel Vaucaire, and Pierre Noriey, Histoire de la Troisième République. Paris, 1935.

Godfrey, James L., "Alphonse Aulard (1849–1928)," in B. E. Schmitt, ed., Some Historians of Modern Europe: Essays in Historiography by Former Students of the Department of History of the University of Chicago, Chicago, 1942, pp. 45–65.

Gooch, G. P., History and Historians in the Nineteenth Century. 2d ed., London, 1913.

Gottschalk, Louis R., "The French Revolution: Conspiracy or Circumstance?," in Persecution or Liberty: Essays in Honor of George Lincoln Burr, New York, 1931, pp. 445–72.

Guérard, Albert L., French Civilization in the Nineteenth Century: A Historical Introduction. New York, 1914.

Hale, Richard W., Jr., Democratic France: The Third Republic from Sedan to Vichy. New York, 1941.

Halévy, Daniel, Essais sur le mouvement ouvrier en France. Paris, 1901.

——— La Fin des notables. 2 vols., Paris, 1930–1937.

Hanotaux, Gabriel, Contemporary France. Eng. trans., 4 vols., London, 1903–1909.

Hayes, Carlton J. H., France: A Nation of Patriots. New York, 1930. In Social and Economic Studies of Post-War France, ed. by C. J. H. Hayes.

———— A Generation of Materialism: 1871–1890. New York, 1942. In The Rise of Modern Europe series, ed. by W. L. Langer.

Hyndman, H. M., Clemenceau: The Man and His Times. New York, 1919.

Janet, P., Philosophie de la Révolution française. 4th ed., Paris, 1892.

Jellinek, Frank, The Paris Commune of 1871. London, 1937.

Kelso, Maxwell R., "The Inception of the Modern French Labor Movement, 1871–1879: A Reappraisal," *Journal of Modern History,* VIII (1936), 173–93.

Kuczynski, Jürgen, Labour Conditions in Western Europe: 1820–1935. New York, 1937.

Labusquière, John, La Troisième République: 1871–1900. Vol. XII of Histoire socialiste: 1789–1900, ed. by Jean Jaurès. Paris, 1907.

Lajusan, A., "Les origines de la Troisième République: quelques éclaircissements, 1871–1876," *Revue d'histoire moderne,* V (1930), 419–38.

Laronze, Georges, Histoire de la Commune de 1871, d'après des documents et des souvenirs inédits: la justice. Paris, 1928.

Leighton, John, Paris under the Commune. London, 1871.

Levasseur, Emile, Questions ouvrières et industrielles sous la Troisième République. Paris, 1907.

Lewinsky, Ernst, Thiers und der Pakt von Bordeaux. Berlin, 1927.

Lhéritier, Michel, La France depuis 1870. Paris, 1922.

Lissagaray, P. O., History of the Commune of 1871. Trans. by E. M. Aveling. London, 1886.

Lorwin, Louis, Syndicalism in France. New York, 1914. 2d rev. ed. of The Labor Movement in France, No. 116 in Studies in History, Economics, and Public Law of Columbia University.

Louis, Paul, Histoire de la classe ouvrière en France de la Révolution à nos jours: la condition matérielle des travailleurs, les salaires et la coût de la vie. Paris, 1927.

———— Histoire du parti socialiste en France: 1871–1914. Paris, 1922.

Marcère, M. de, Le Seize-mai et la fin du septennat. Paris, 1900.

March, Lucien, "Le mouvement des prix et l'activité productrice," *Bulletin de la Statistique générale de la France,* vol. I (1911).

March, Thomas, History of the Paris Commune of 1871. London, 1896.

Mason, E. S., The Paris Commune: An Episode in the History of the Socialist Movement. New York, 1930.

Moon, Parker Thomas, The Labor Problem and the Social Catholic Movement in France: A Study in the History of Social Politics. New York, 1921.

Muret, Charlotte T., French Royalist Doctrines since the Revolution. New York, 1933.

Ogburn, William F., and William Jaffé, The Economic Development of Post-War France: A Survey of Production. New York, 1929. In Social and Economic Studies of Post-War France series, ed. by C. J. H. Hayes.

Petit, Maxime, with the collaboration of Auguste Dupouy, Henri Froidevaux, General Ibos, Francisque Marotte, Olivier Martin, Albert Pingaud, Emile Sedeyn, Histoire de France: la Troisième République. Paris, 1936.

Pipkin, Charles W., Social Politics and Modern Democracies. 2 vols., Vol. II: New York, 1931.

Pressac, Pierre de, Les Forces historiques de la France: la tradition dans l'orientation politique des provinces. Paris, 1928.

Prolo, Jacques, Les Anarchistes. Vol. X of Histoire des partis socialistes en France, ed. by A. Zévaès. Paris, 1912.

Reclus, Maurice, Le Seize-mai. Paris, 1931.

Recouly, Raymond. The Third Republic. Trans. by E. F. Buckley. London. 1928. In The National History of France series, ed. by F. Funck-Brentano.

Reinach, Joseph, Histoire de l'affaire Dreyfus. 7 vols., Paris, 1901–1911.

Roepke, Fritz, Von Gambetta bis Clemenceau: fünfzig Jahre französischer Politik und Geschichte. Stuttgart and Berlin, 1922.

Saposs, David, The Labor Movement in Post-War France. New York, 1931. In Social and Economic Studies of Post-War France series, ed. by C. J. H. Hayes.

Schmitt, B. E., ed., Some Historians of Modern Europe: Essays in Historiography by Former Students of the Department of History of the University of Chicago. Chicago, 1942.

Seignobos, Charles, Le Déclin de l'Empire et l'établissement de la Troisième République: 1859–1875. Vol. VII of Histoire de la France contemporaine depuis la Révolution jusqu'à la paix de 1919, ed. by Ernest Lavisse. Paris, 1921.

———— L'Evolution de la Troisième République. Paris, 1921. Vol. VIII of Histoire de la France contemporaine depuis la Révolution jusqu'à la paix de 1919, ed. by Ernest Lavisse.

Soltau, Roger H., French Parties and Politics: 1871–1921. London, 1922.

———— French Political Thought in the Nineteenth Century. New Haven, 1931.

Thorp, Willard L., Business Annals. New York, 1926.

Weill, Georges, Histoire du mouvement social en France: 1852–1902. Paris, 1904.

Weinstein, Harold R., Jean Jaurès: A Study of Patriotism in the French Socialist Movement. New York, 1936.

Winnacker, R. A., "Bibliographical Article: The Third French Republic, 1870–1914," *Journal of Modern History*, X (1938), 372–409.

—— "The French Election of 1871," *Papers of the Michigan Academy of Science, Arts and Letters*, XXII (1938), 473–83.

Zévaès, Alexander, Aperçu historique sur le Parti ouvrier français. Lille, 1899.

—— Au Temps du Boulangisme. 5th ed., Paris, 1930.

—— Au Temps du Seize-mai. Paris, 1932.

—— De la Semaine sanglante au Congrès de Marseilles: 1871–1879. Paris, 1911. Vol. II of Histoire des partis socialistes en France, ed. by A. Zévaès.

—— Les Guesdistes. Paris, 1911. Vol. III of Histoire des partis socialistes en France, ed. by A. Zévaès.

—— Histoire de la Troisième République: 1870–1926. Paris, 1926.

—— Le Socialisme en France depuis 1871. Paris, 1908.

INDEX